Real Time

Software Testing

Interview

Questions and Answers

By : Anand Hooda

Anand Hooda Classes
YouTube

Copyright

All rights reserved. No part of this book may be reproduced, stored in a retrieval system, or transmitted in any form or by any means, without the prior written permission of the author, except in the case of brief quotations embedded in critical articles or reviews.
Every effort has been made in the preparation of this book to ensure the accuracy of the information presented.

If someone use the content of the book in photocopy, video, online uploading etc. then in that case judicial action will take place against him/her. Rohtak (Haryana) will be only Judicial place.

This book is dedicated to **my Loving Daughters**

Table of Contents

Question 45. As a Test Manager, how do you handle delays or changes in the schedule?

Question 46. Can you call the base class method without creating an object?

Question 47. How do you iterate over the map?

Question 48. What's the difference between HashMap and Hashtable?

Question 49. Difference between String, StringBuffer and StringBuilder in table form with example?

Question: 50. Can you have overloaded constructors in the same class?

Question 51. Can we override the constructor? If not then Why?

Question 52. What is the default constructor? Where we use default constructor?

Question 53. How to get a number of elements in ArrayList?

Question 54. What is the difference between XPath and CSS? Which one is faster and why?

Question 55. How to handle dynamic element in Automation?

Question 56. How do you deal with stale element exceptions in Selenium?

Question 57: What is RFP and component of it? Have you been involved in it?

Question 58: What are the various contents of Test Plan?

Question 59: According to you What is expected from Testing Team when a software needs to test?

Question 60. On Which port Htpp and Htpps are tested?

Question 61. How do you define the format of writing a good test case?

Question 62. If you had to execute a big suite in a small window of time, how would you do it?

Question 63. Java Program to reverse the element of an Array without the use of the reverse method?

Question 64. Java Program to count the characters in the string (How many a, how many b, like this)?

Question 65. Java Program to count the Words in the String (like: How many Anand , how many Hooda like this)?

Question 66. Java Program to count the element in the a List?

Question 67. Java Program to find the duplicate elements from the ArrayList?

Question 68. Java Program to remove the duplicate elements from the ArrayList?

Question 69. Java Program to find the Factorial of a number?

Question 70. Java Program to find the even and odd number in the List?

Question 71. Java Program to reverse the String?

Question 72. Java Program to find the Second shortest element in the Array?

Question 73. Java Program to find the size of an ArrayList?

Question 74. Java Program to sort the element of an Array?

Question 75. Java Program to find the elements that start and end with same Char in an ArrayList?

Question 76. Java Program to find the elements (Strings) that have length more than 8 in an ArrayList?

Question 77. Java Program to find out the Sum of a number and also find count digit in the number?

Question 78. Java Program to find out the common elements from two Arrays?

Question 79. Java Program to find out the length of longest String in an Array?

Question 80. Java Program to find out the sum of all elements in Array?

Question 81. Java Program to find out the average all elements in Array?

Question 82. Java Program to find out the square of each and every element in Array?

Question 83. Java Program to find out the minimum and maximum number in Array?

Question 1. What is test strategy?

Answer: A test strategy is a high-level document that outlines the approach, scope, resources, and schedule for testing within a project or organization.

Always remember that Test Strategy is a static document and it is created by Test manager.

It serves as a roadmap that defines how testing will be conducted and how various testing activities will be carried out to achieve the quality objectives of the project.

A test strategy typically includes the **following components:**

1) **Objectives and Scope:** Defines the goals, objectives, and the extent of testing in terms of features, functionalities, and systems to be tested.

2) **Test Approach:** Describes the overall testing approach, including methodologies, techniques, and tools that will be utilized during the testing process. It may detail whether the testing will be manual, automated, or a combination of both.

3) **Test Environment:** Specifies the necessary hardware, software, and other resources needed for testing. This involves details about test environments, configurations, and data.

4) **Test deliverables:** Lists the documentation and artifacts that will be produced during testing, such as test plans, test cases, test scripts, test reports, and defect reports.

5) **Test Phases:** Outlines the different stages or phases of testing (such as unit testing, integration testing, system testing, etc.) and their objectives.

6) **Entry and Exit Criteria:** Defines the conditions to begin and end each phase of testing. Entry criteria might include prerequisites to start testing, while exit criteria signify when testing is considered complete for a particular phase.

7) **Risks and Contingencies:** Identifies potential risks, issues, and mitigation plans in case of unforeseen circumstances impacting testing activities.

8) **Roles and Responsibilities:** Clarifies the responsibilities of individuals involved in the testing process, including test managers, testers, developers, stakeholders, and others.

9) **Metrics and Reporting:** Specifies the metrics and key performance indicators (KPIs) used to measure the effectiveness of testing and how progress and results will be reported to stakeholders.

10) **Review and Approval Processes:** Describes how the test strategy will be reviewed, updated, and approved, ensuring that it aligns with the project's objectives and requirements.

Question 2. How many scrum meetings are held in the team?

Answer: The main Scrum meetings are as follows:

1) **Sprint Planning:** This meeting marks the start of a sprint and involves the entire Scrum team. The team collaborates to determine what work will be undertaken during the sprint and how it will be achieved.
2) **Daily Stand-up (Daily Scrum):** Held every day during the sprint, this short meeting involves all team members discussing their progress, what they've accomplished since the last stand-up, what they plan to do before the next meeting, and any impediments they are facing.

3) **Sprint Review:** Conducted at the end of the sprint, the Sprint Review involves the team demonstrating the completed work to stakeholders and receiving feedback. The goal is to gather input that will help in adapting the product backlog.
4) **Sprint Retrospective:** Also held at the end of the sprint, the Sprint Retrospective involves the team reflecting on the past sprint to identify what went well, what could be improved, and how to implement those improvements in the next sprint.

Question 3. Test Manager Responsibilities?

Answer: By asking this question employer wants to know what you have done in your previous organization with your role. Hiring managers also want to get a sense that, do you have the same role & Responsibilities they are looking for.

Always remember that QA/Test Manager Roles & Responsibilities vary from organization to organization.

Following are some common Roles & Responsibilities:

1. Evaluate customer requirements and ensure that these are met in the QA plans and standards.
2. Communicate quality standards to the QA team, product development team, and other stakeholders.
3. Estimate/Plan QA effort and manage QA resources on various projects. Review resource bookings and course assignments to have a view on the team's utilization.
4. Manage the QA efforts for all of the QA projects teams at the company/org / group
5. Build a great team - identify, interview, and hire the best resources Provide mentorship and coaching to help individual QA engineers grow in their careers and maximize their impact.
6. Implement and maintain tools and processes for testing
7. Define the test strategy to be applied based on the best practices and project specificities
8. Ensure content and structure of all testing documents/artefacts is documented and maintained
9. Document, implement, monitor, and enforce all processes for testing as per the standards defined by the organization
10. Keep track of the new requirements/changes of the Project
11. Organize the status meetings and share the Status Report (Daily, Weekly etc.) with stakeholders
12. Act as the single point of contact between Release Manager, Development and Testers
13. Prepare and track the report of testing activities like: testing results, Testing Reports, test case coverage, resources requirement, defects discovered and their status, performance baselines etc.
14. Prepare requirements analysis, create, and review test plans, write test cases/scripts.
15. Create and manage automation framework. Define different methods and procedures for test automation of Web and mobile applications.
16. Review customer feedback and complaints or defect trends. Analyse data to find areas of improvement, particularly where problems recur.
17. Assist functional leads in root cause analysis where needed.
18. Create dashboards and reports for the overall Quality health of the courses. Review test execution reports and charts regularly to simplify and make easily usable.
19. Develops, implements, and manages processes to ensure that products meet required
20. specifications for quality, function, and reliability prior to delivery.
21. Identifies and sets appropriate quality standards and parameters for products.
22. Communicates quality standards and parameters to QA team, product development team, and other appropriate staff.
23. Works with Project Managers to develop project schedules and resource allocation models for QA related projects and other activities such as software deployment, customer integration, and professional services validation.

24. Coordinate product testing processes.
25. Participates in product testing.
26. Identifies and analyses issues, bugs, defects, and other problems, particularly when problems recur in multiple products; recommends and facilitates solutions to these issues.
27. Review client, customer, and user feedback.
28. Maintains compliance with federal, state, local, and organizational laws, regulations, guidelines, and policies.

Question 4. How to check and test http/https request and response for a website?

Answer: Testing HTTP/HTTPS requests and responses for a website involves various techniques and tools to ensure that the website functions correctly, handles requests properly, and provides appropriate responses. Here are steps and tools you can use to test HTTP/HTTPS requests and responses:

1. **Manual Testing:**

   a) **Browser Developer Tools:** Most modern browsers have built-in developer tools that allow you to inspect network requests and responses. Use these tools (e.g., Chrome DevTools, Firefox Developer Tools) to monitor HTTP/HTTPS traffic, view headers, status codes, and response payloads.

2. **Automated Testing:**

   a) **API Testing Tools:** Tools like Postman, Insomnia, or cURL allow you to craft HTTP requests and inspect the responses. They provide a user-friendly interface for sending requests, examining headers, and reviewing JSON/XML responses.
   b) **Automated Testing Frameworks:** Selenium, Cypress, or Puppeteer (for headless browser testing) can be used to automate HTTP/HTTPS request-response validation in functional tests, especially for web applications.
   c) **Load Testing Tools:** Tools like JMeter or Gatling can simulate heavy loads on a server by sending a large number of HTTP requests. These can test how the website handles concurrent requests and responses under load.

3. **Security and Performance Testing:**

   a) **Security Testing Tools:** Use tools like OWASP ZAP or Burp Suite to test for security vulnerabilities, including common web application vulnerabilities (SQL injection, XSS, CSRF, etc.).

   b) **Performance Testing Tools:** Tools like Apache JMeter, LoadRunner, or Gatling can test website performance by simulating various load scenarios, measuring response times, and identifying bottlenecks.

4. **Checklist for HTTP/HTTPS Testing:**

   a) Ensure that the website handles both HTTP and HTTPS requests appropriately.
   b) Validate correct status codes (e.g., 200 OK, 404 Not Found, 500 Internal Server Error) for different scenarios.
   c) Verify response payloads for correctness and consistency according to the API or web application specifications.

d) Test for edge cases, boundary values, and error conditions to validate the website's robustness and error-handling capabilities.

e) Verify that the website securely handles sensitive data over HTTPS, ensuring encryption, and appropriate certificate validation.

Question 5. How you will do https testing?

Answer: Testing HTTPS (Hypertext Transfer Protocol Secure) involves verifying the secure transmission of data between a client (such as a web browser) and a server.

Here are steps and methods to conduct HTTPS testing:

1) **Certificate Validation:** Ensure that the website uses a valid SSL/TLS certificate. Check the certificate's expiration date, issuer, and whether it's properly signed by a trusted Certificate Authority.

2) **Protocol Version:** Test the supported SSL/TLS protocol versions (SSL 3.0, TLS 1.0, 1.1, 1.2, 1.3) and verify that the website is configured to use the latest secure versions.

3) **Cipher Suites:** Verify the supported cipher suites to ensure they are secure and follow best practices. Avoid using weak or deprecated ciphers.

4) **Mixed Content:** Check for mixed content warnings. Ensure that all resources (images, scripts, stylesheets, etc.) are served over HTTPS to prevent browser warnings and maintain security.

5) **HTTP to HTTPS Redirects:** Test whether HTTP URLs redirect to their HTTPS counterparts. Any HTTP request should automatically be redirected to the HTTPS version of the URL.

6) **Security Headers:** Validate the presence and correctness of security headers like Strict-Transport-Security (HSTS), Content Security Policy (CSP), X-Content-Type-Options, X-Frame-Options, and others. These headers enhance the security posture of the website.

7) **Secure Data Transmission:** Verify that sensitive information (user credentials, payment details, personal data) is transmitted securely over HTTPS and that there are no mixed-content warnings or insecure content.

8) **Man-in-the-Middle (MITM) Attacks:** Perform tests to ensure the website is protected against common MITM attacks, such as eavesdropping or data manipulation during transmission.

9) **Robustness Against Attacks:** Use tools to simulate and test common HTTPS vulnerabilities and attacks like BEAST, POODLE, Heartbleed, and others to check the website's resilience.

10) **Automated Scanning Tools:** Utilize security scanning tools (such as OWASP ZAP, Qualys SSL Labs, SSLyze) to automatically test for SSL/TLS configuration issues, certificate problems, and vulnerabilities.

11) **Manual Testing:** Manually inspect HTTPS implementation using web browser developer tools to analyze network traffic, certificate details, and security information.

12) **By Automation Script:** By using of **desired capabilities**

Capabilities is an interface in WebDriver library whose direct implementation is Desired Capabilities class. In simple word Desired Capabilities is a class which helps us to customize our browser. Desired Capabilities help to set properties for web Driver.

Desired Capabilities is a series of value / Key pairs that stores browser properties like browser name, version and the path of the browser driver in the system etc. to determine the behavior of the browser at run time.

Desired Capabilities can also be used to configure the driver object of Selenium WebDriver like Firefox Driver, Chrome Driver etc.

Some of the default capabilities that are common across browsers are shown in the following

table:

Capability	What it is used for
takesScreenShot	Tells whether the browser session can take a screenshot of the webpage
handlesAlert	Tells whether the browser session can handle modal dialogs
cssSelectorsEnabled	Tells whether the browser session can use CSS selectors while searching for elements
javascriptEnabled	Enables/disables user-supplied JavaScript execution in the context of the webpage
acceptSSLCerts	Enables/disables the browser to accept all of the SSL certificates by default
webStorageEnabled	This is an HTML5 feature, and it is possible to enable or disable the browser session to interact with storage objects

What is SSL Certification?

SSL (Secure Sockets Layer) is a standard security protocol for establishing a secure connection between the server and the client which is a browser.

When we hit a URL on browser & we get a window / page that have following massage like: "site security certification is not trusted", "this site is not properly you looking for", "connection is not private" etc. See the below diagram to understand well.

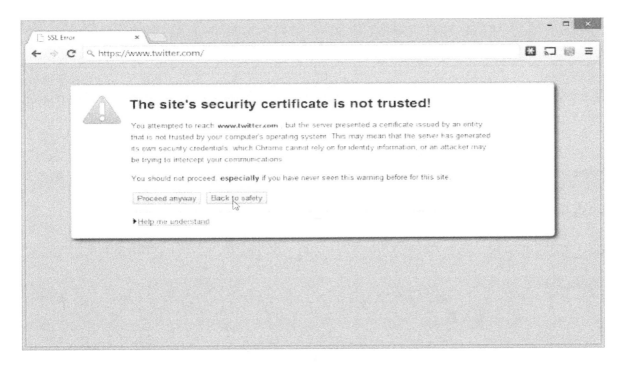

So on these types of windows / Page we have to select and click on proceed, proceed anyway, Advance & proceed.

How to handle SSL Certification in Selenium?

To handle this we have to add some code in our browser. By this code Selenium WebDriver automatically understand that page and click on "Proceed" & navigate to the next page.

To handle certification on any browser (Chrome in this case) we have two things

A. General Chrome Profile
B. Existing (local browser) on our machine

We need to merge both profiles to handle SSL-Certification, i.e. we have to merge General Chrome Profile with local browser.

To do this we have to do the following steps:

a) First all create the object of Desired Capabilities class like this:

DesiredCapabilities ch = new DesiredCapabilities.chrome();

b) Second use the ChromeOptions class & create object of it. like:

ChromeOptions co = new ChromeOptions();

c) Third, we have to merge general chrome profile characteristics with local browser. So to merge both we have to pass all general chrome profile characteristics to local browser like this

co-merge (ch);

d) Fourth, After this do same as you do in diff programs like.

//System.setProperty("webdriver.chrome.driver", "/AnandData/library/chromedriver"); //for mac

System.setProperty("webdriver.chrome.driver", "/AnandData/library/chromedr iver.exe");//window

WebDriver driver = new ChromeDriver();

e) Fifth, we have to call the local Chrome Option to our Selenium browser, means to call the Chrome Option on our Selenium browser we have to call the object of Chrome

Option class to our WebDriver. By this way we are creating a linking between Chrome Option class & WebDriver.

WebDriver driver = new Chrome Driver (co);

f) As you do all things in a proper manner your browser will handle the SSL-certification. Program:

public class SSLCerification {

@Test

public void OpenUrl() {

DesiredCapabilities ch = new DesiredCapabilities.chrome(); /

/ch.acceptInsecureCerts(); // we can also use this
ch.setCapability(CapabilityType.ACCEPT_INSECURE_CERTS, true);

ch.setCapability(CapabilityType.ACCEPT_SSL_CERTS, true);

ChromeOptions co = new ChromeOptions();
co.merge(ch);

System.setProperty("webdriver.chrome.driver", "/AnandData/library/chromedriver ")
WebDriver driver = new ChromeDriver(co);

driver.get("https://jqueryui.com/droppable/");
driver.manage().timeouts().implicitlyWait(30,TimeUnit.SECONDS); driver.manage().window().maximize();

}}

Note: we can also handle to insecure certification in diff. way that is

ch.setCapability(CapabilityType.ACCEPT_INSECURE_CERTS,

ch.setCapability(CapabilityType.ACCEPT_SSL_CERTS, true); Similarly, we can add diff certification here.

Question 6. How do you calculate effort Estimation for testing with respect to developer in Agile?

Answer: In Agile methodologies, calculating effort estimation for testing in relation to development involves a more iterative and collaborative approach between the testing and development teams. Here are some steps to calculate effort estimation for testing concerning the developers in an Agile context:

1) **Story Points or Relative Sizing:** Agile teams often use story points for estimating effort. During backlog refinement or Sprint Planning, both developers and testers discuss user stories and collectively assign story points. This ensures that the testing effort is considered alongside the development effort.

2) **Collaborative Estimation:** Engage in collaborative estimation sessions where developers and testers jointly estimate the effort needed for testing tasks associated with a user story. Use techniques like Planning Poker where team members discuss and collectively agree on the estimation.

3) **Consider Testing Tasks:** Identify testing tasks associated with each user story or feature during Sprint Planning. Estimate the effort required for tasks such as test case creation, execution, regression testing, exploratory testing, automation, and defect management.

4) **Define Acceptance Criteria:** Ensure that acceptance criteria are well-defined and agreed upon by both developers and testers. These criteria help in determining when a user story is complete and ready for release.

5) **Testing Dependencies and Impact:** Consider dependencies on development tasks and the impact they may have on testing. For instance, if the development of a particular feature is delayed, it might affect the testing effort for that feature.

6) **Keep Estimations Relative:** The goal is to have relative estimations rather than precise figures. Focus on understanding the relative complexity and effort compared to other tasks or stories.

7) **Frequent Refinement and Review:** review and refine estimations during Sprint Retrospectives or as new information becomes available. Testers and developers should collaborate to reassess and adjust the estimates based on the evolving project dynamics.

8) **Use Historical Data:** Leverage historical data from previous Sprints or projects to make more informed estimations. Understanding how similar tasks were completed in the past helps in providing more accurate estimations.

9) **Buffer for Unforeseen Work:** Allocate a percentage of the Sprint capacity for unforeseen testing tasks or unexpected issues that might arise during the Sprint.

10) **Visualize and Track Effort:** Use Agile tools like Scrum boards, Kanban boards, or task boards to visualize and track testing tasks alongside development tasks, allowing for transparency and better coordination.

11) **Encourage Continuous Communication:** Maintain constant communication between developers and testers throughout the Sprint to ensure alignment and to address any discrepancies or changes in requirements that might affect effort estimations.

For Example: If a developer spends 100 hours developing a functionality, a common approximation in Agile settings could be that the testing effort might range from approximately 30 to 40 hours,

Question 7. What is your role in Agile as Test Manager/ What is role of Test Manger in Agile?

Answer: In Agile environments, the traditional hierarchical Test Manager role might be distributed among the team or transformed into a coaching or facilitation role.

Agile principles emphasize collaboration, self-organization, and shared responsibility. Therefore, the Test Manager often serves as a facilitator, mentor, and a contributor to the overall testing strategy within the Agile team, working closely with developers, product owners, and other stakeholders to ensure quality and timely delivery, there are still essential responsibilities and contributions within an Agile environment:

1) **Test Strategy and Planning:** The Test Manager collaborates with the Agile team to establish a test strategy and plan that aligns with Agile principles. They help define testing objectives, guidelines, and approaches that best fit the Agile project.

2) **Resource Allocation:** Although not in the traditional sense of assigning tasks, the Test Manager can guide the team in understanding the necessary testing resources and skill sets required for successful delivery. This might involve identifying training needs or areas for skill enhancement within the testing team.

3) **Testing Expertise and Guidance:** Offering guidance and mentoring to the testing team is vital. The Test Manager assists in maintaining testing best practices, providing support in solving complex testing challenges, and ensuring quality standards are met.

4) **Collaboration and Communication:** Facilitating communication between the testing team and other Agile team members is crucial. The Test Manager ensures that testing objectives are well understood and that any impediments or challenges are communicated effectively.

5) **Test Metrics and Reporting:** Tracking and reporting on testing progress, quality metrics, and key performance indicators to stakeholders and the team is a significant responsibility. The Test Manager helps to ensure that the necessary metrics are captured and communicated effectively.

6) **Test Environment and Tools:** The Test Manager oversees the setup and maintenance of the test environment and tools. Ensuring that the team has the necessary tools and environments to perform testing is vital for a successful Agile project.

7) **Continuous Improvement:** Encouraging a culture of continuous improvement within the testing team is important. The Test Manager can facilitate retrospectives and encourage the team to reflect on testing processes, identify improvements, and implement changes accordingly.

8) **Adaptability and Flexibility:** Being adaptable and flexible is key in Agile projects. The Test Manager may need to adjust strategies, plans, and resource allocations based on the changing project requirements and priorities.

Question 8. How to manage Automation Testing parallelly in an Agile Sprint?

Answer: Managing automation testing in parallel with development during an Agile Sprint is a critical aspect of Agile testing. It ensures that automated tests keep pace with the development work and helps maintain a continuous integration and delivery (CI/CD) pipeline. Here are steps to manage automation testing in parallel with development in an Agile Sprint:

1) **Early Involvement in Sprint Planning:** Automation testing should be considered from the beginning of the Sprint. Involve automation testers in Sprint planning sessions to understand the user stories and testing requirements.

2) **Identify Automation Scope:** Determine the scope of automation for each sprint based on the priority of features or functionalities. Focus on automating tests that offer high business value or are integral to the product.

3) **Test Case Identification and Prioritization and script writing:** Identify test cases suitable for automation and prioritize them based on their importance and potential for regression. Start with critical, repetitive, or time-consuming test cases.

4) **Continuous Integration and Builds:** Integrate automated tests into the continuous integration process. Trigger automated tests as part of the build pipeline to run on each code commit or build.

5) **Parallel Execution and CI/CD Pipelines:** Set up your automation tests to run in parallel, utilizing different test environments and configurations, to save time. Incorporate them into the CI/CD pipeline to ensure they run automatically.

6) **Retrospectives:** Include automation efforts in Sprint retrospectives. Discuss challenges and areas for improvement, and make adjustments as needed.

Note: If we don't have much time to automate in the same sprint then at least we can create feature file and Step-definition files for the functionalities.

Question 9. What Security Testing do you perform for a website?

Answer: Security testing for a website involves evaluating its security measures and identifying vulnerabilities that could potentially be exploited by malicious actors. The specific security testing activities can vary based on the website's nature, its technologies, and its risk profile. Here are some common security testing activities performed for websites:

1) **Vulnerability Assessment and Scanning:** Automated scanning tools, such as Nessus, OpenVAS, or Qualys, can be used to identify known vulnerabilities in the website, including outdated software, misconfigurations, and common security issues.

2) **Penetration Testing (Pen Testing):** Engage ethical hackers to simulate real-world attacks on the website. Penetration testing uncovers vulnerabilities that automated tools may miss, providing a more comprehensive assessment.

3) **Cross-Site Scripting (XSS) Testing:** Check for the presence of XSS vulnerabilities, where malicious scripts can be injected into the website, potentially compromising user data.

4) **SQL Injection Testing:** Identify SQL injection vulnerabilities, which can allow attackers to manipulate a website's database and steal sensitive information.

5) **Cross-Site Request Forgery (CSRF) Testing:** Evaluate the website's resistance to CSRF attacks, which can trick users into performing actions without their consent.
6) **Security Headers Assessment:** Check for the presence and correct configuration of security headers like Content Security Policy (CSP), X-Content-Type-Options, and HTTP Strict Transport Security (HSTS).

7) **Authentication and Authorization Testing:** Assess the effectiveness of user authentication and authorization mechanisms, including password policies, session management, and role-based access controls.

8) **Secure File Upload Testing:** Test for vulnerabilities related to file uploads, which can be exploited to execute malicious code or upload malicious files.

9) **SSL/TLS Certificate Assessment:** Ensure that SSL/TLS certificates are correctly configured and up to date to protect data in transit.

10) **Security Patch and Update Verification:** Regularly verify that all software, libraries, and frameworks used in the website are updated to the latest secure versions to avoid known vulnerabilities.

11) **API Security Testing:** Assess the security of APIs (Application Programming Interfaces) used by the website to ensure that they are protected from unauthorized access and data breaches.

12) **Data Privacy Testing:** Check for data leakage and privacy issues, especially in forms, cookies, and other data transmission mechanisms.

13) **Session Management Testing:** Ensure that session tokens and cookies are securely managed, preventing session fixation, session hijacking, and other session-related vulnerabilities.

14) **Content Security Testing:** Review the website's content, including user-generated content, to prevent content-based attacks, such as defacement or harmful uploads.

15) **Distributed Denial of Service (DDoS) Testing:** Assess the website's resilience against DDoS attacks, which can disrupt the availability of the site.

16) **Security Documentation Review:** Evaluate the presence and quality of security documentation, including incident response plans, security policies, and guidelines for developers.

Automated Security Testing Tools:

1) **Nessus:** An automated vulnerability scanner that identifies security issues, misconfigurations, and known vulnerabilities in the network and web applications.

2) **Burp Suite:** A comprehensive web application security testing tool that includes both automated scanning and manual testing capabilities. It's particularly effective for web application vulnerability assessment.

3) **OWASP ZAP (Zed Attack Proxy):** An open-source web application security scanner used for finding security vulnerabilities in web applications. It has both automated and manual penetration testing features.

4) **Acunetix:** A web vulnerability scanner that automates security testing and provides comprehensive scanning for web applications, detecting a wide range of vulnerabilities.

5) **SQLMap:** While partially automated, SQLMap is a powerful tool used for automated SQL injection detection and exploitation. It can be used for both automated and manual testing.

6) **Qualys:** A cloud-based security and compliance platform that performs vulnerability assessments across web applications, networks, and databases.

<u>Manual Security Testing Tools:</u>

1) **Burp Suite (Manual Features):** Apart from its automated scanning capabilities, Burp Suite offers various manual testing tools for manipulating, intercepting, and analyzing HTTP requests and responses, along with advanced testing features.

2) **Nmap (Network Mapper):** While mainly an automated tool, Nmap also offers manual features for network scanning, identification of hosts, services, and potential security issues.

3) **Wireshark:** A network protocol analyzer that assists in manual security analysis by capturing and inspecting packets, helping in identifying network vulnerabilities.

4) **Metasploit:** Offers both automated and manual penetration testing tools for identifying security weaknesses and launching exploit campaigns against web applications.

5) **Browser Developer Tools:** Chrome Developer Tools, Firefox Developer Tools, and similar browser-based tools allow manual inspection of network requests, manipulation of data, and testing security features directly in the browser.

6) **Zed Attack Proxy (ZAP):** ZAP from OWASP includes features for both automated and manual web application security testing, offering a wide array of tools for manual testing and analysis.

<u>Which tool is best:</u>

The "best" tool often depends on various factors, including:

1) **Type of Testing Needed:** Some tools specialize in certain types of security testing, such as SQL injection or cross-site scripting. Choose based on the specific vulnerabilities you want to detect.

2) **Ease of Use:** Consider the tool's user interface, reporting capabilities, and ease of setup and integration with existing systems.

3) **Customization and Flexibility:** Look for tools that allow for flexibility in customizing tests and adapting to different testing scenarios.

4) **Community Support and Updates:** Tools backed by active communities and regular updates often provide more reliable results and keep up with the latest vulnerabilities.

5) **Compliance and Reporting:** If regulatory compliance is a concern, consider tools that offer comprehensive reporting and compliance features.

Question 10. What challenges do you face in Agile Testing?

Answer: In Agile testing, various challenges can arise due to the nature of the Agile methodology. Some of these challenges include:

1) **Short Timeframes for Testing:** Agile emphasizes short development cycles or sprints, which can limit the time available for comprehensive testing. It can be challenging to ensure adequate test coverage within these tight timelines.

2) **Frequent Changes and Uncertainty:** Requirements often evolve and change throughout the project. Adapting to these changes while ensuring continuous testing coverage and maintaining test documentation can be demanding.

3) **Parallel Development and Testing:** Coordinating testing activities alongside ongoing development can be challenging. Ensuring synchronization between development teams and testing teams to avoid bottlenecks requires effective communication and collaboration.

4) **Continuous Integration and Deployment (CI/CD):** Integrating testing into the CI/CD pipeline is crucial in Agile. Challenges can arise in setting up and maintaining automated testing, ensuring its reliability, and adjusting tests for frequent builds and deployments.

5) **Test Automation Challenges:** While test automation is integral in Agile, challenges include initial setup time, maintenance of automated scripts, and ensuring they remain relevant as the application evolves.

6) **Resource Allocation:** Ensuring the availability of skilled testing resources within the Agile team is crucial. Sometimes, there might be a shortage of testing resources or a skill gap within the team.

7) **Quality vs. Speed Balancing Act:** Agile's focus on rapid iterations might sometimes prioritize speed over comprehensive testing. Balancing speed and quality becomes a challenge, especially when pressured to deliver within strict timelines.

8) **Regression Testing:** As new features are added or modified in each sprint, ensuring that these changes do not impact existing functionalities (regression testing) within the short sprint cycles can be a challenge.

9) **Test Documentation and Knowledge Transfer:** Creating and maintaining test documentation, as well as sharing knowledge among team members, can be challenging in the context of rapid changes and iterations.

10) **Scaling Agile Testing:** As the project grows or when multiple Agile teams are involved, scaling Agile testing to maintain quality across different teams or projects can be complex.

Question 11. List of Scenario to test the e-commerce retail testing especially Smoke Scenario?

Answer:

E-commerce Website Scenarios: Testing an e-commerce website involves examining a wide range of functionalities and scenarios to ensure a seamless and secure user experience. Here's a comprehensive list of scenarios to consider for testing an e-commerce platform:

1) **User Registration and Authentication:**
   a) Verify user registration with valid and invalid credentials.
   b) Test the login functionality with correct and incorrect login credentials.
   c) Test the 'Forgot Password' functionality for password recovery.

2) **Product Browsing and Search:**
   a) Verify search functionality with various search criteria.
   b) Test category navigation and accurate product filtering.
   c) Verify product listing, descriptions, images, and prices.

3) **Shopping Cart and Checkout:**
   a) Test adding, updating, and removing items from the shopping cart.
   b) Validate multiple payment options.
   c) Verify the checkout process, including billing and shipping information.

4) **Payment Gateway Testing:**
   a) Test different payment methods - credit/debit cards, PayPal, etc.
   b) Verify secure and encrypted transactions.
   c) Test for successful and failed transaction scenarios.

5) **Order Management:**
   a) Test order placement, cancellation, and modification.
   b) Verify order status tracking and confirmation emails.
   c) Test for multiple shipping and delivery options.

6) **Reviews and Ratings:**
   a) Test the functionality to add, view, and delete product reviews.
   b) Ensure ratings and reviews display accurately on product pages.

7) **Wishlist and Favourites:**
   a) Test adding and removing items from the Wishlist.
   b) Verify if Wishlist items persist across user sessions.

8) **Discounts and Promotions:**
   a) Verify the application of discounts and promo codes.
   b) Test various discount scenarios and their application in the checkout process.

9) **Email Notifications:**
   a) Validate order confirmation, shipping updates, and promotional emails.
   b) Test the unsubscribe functionality from promotional emails.

10) **Security and Privacy:**
   a) Ensure secure transactions using HTTPS and SSL certificates.
   b) Test user data protection and compliance with data privacy regulations.

11) **Mobile Responsiveness and Compatibility:**
   a) Test website functionality and usability across different devices and screen sizes.
   b) Ensure compatibility with various web browsers and mobile devices.

12) **Performance and Load Testing:**
   a) Test the website's performance under different load conditions.
   b) Ensure the website can handle peak traffic without performance degradation.

13) **Accessibility and Usability:**
   a) Ensure compliance with accessibility standards (WCAG) for users with disabilities.
   b) Verify intuitive and user-friendly navigation and design.

14) **Integration Testing:**

a) Test integrations with third-party services, such as payment gateways, CRM, or shipping carriers.

15) **Cross-Browser Testing:**
   a) Verify website functionality across different web browsers.

Smoke test Scenarios to test the e-commerce website:

Smoke testing involves a quick verification process to ensure that critical functionalities of the system are working without conducting deep or detailed testing.

For an e-commerce website, the following smoke test scenarios can be considered:

1) **Homepage Access and Navigation:**
   a. Verify that the homepage loads properly without errors.
   b. Test basic navigation by clicking essential links, ensuring they direct users to the expected pages.

2) **User Registration and Login:**
   a) Test the user registration functionality.
   b) Verify the login process to ensure users can access their accounts.

3) **Product Search and Listing:**
   a) Ensure the search bar is functional and displays relevant results for common search terms.
   b) Test that product listings display correctly with images, descriptions, and prices.

4) **Adding Items to Cart:**
   a) Verify the functionality to add items to the shopping cart from product pages.
   b) Confirm the cart reflects the added items with correct quantities and prices.

5) **Cart Checkout Process:**
   a) Test the checkout process, ensuring users can proceed from the cart to the checkout page.
   b) Verify users can enter shipping and billing information.

6) **Payment Gateway Access:**
   a) Ensure that the payment gateway is accessible and displays payment options.
   b) Verify the process till the payment page without actual payment processing.

7) **Order Placement Confirmation:**
   a) Test the functionality to confirm orders.
   b) Verify that users receive a confirmation message after placing an order.

8) **Error Handling and Alerts:**
   a) Test the display of error messages and alerts if any critical functionality fails.
   b) Verify that users receive appropriate error messages for failed actions.

9) **Responsiveness Across Devices:**
   a) Test the website's responsiveness across different devices such as desktop, mobile, and tablet.
   b) Ensure that key functionalities work well on various screen sizes.

10) **Link and Image Verification:**
    a) Check that essential images and links on key pages are loading properly.
    b) Verify that links lead to the correct pages and images display correctly.

11) **Navigation Checks:**
    a) Test various navigation elements (menu, categories, footer links) to ensure they lead to the correct pages.

12) **Basic Page Load Speed:**
    a) Check basic load times for the homepage and key category/product pages.
    b) Verify that page's load within an acceptable timeframe.

Question 12. What is Vulnerability Testing?

Answer: Vulnerability testing, also known as vulnerability assessment or vulnerability scanning, is a systematic process of identifying and evaluating security vulnerabilities in software, networks, systems, or web applications.

The primary goal of vulnerability testing is to proactively discover weaknesses in an organization's IT infrastructure before malicious actors can exploit them. These weaknesses may include software flaws, misconfigurations, or other security issues that could be exploited by cyberattacks.

The primary objectives of Vulnerability Testing are:

1) **Identifying Weaknesses:** It aims to discover and pinpoint security weaknesses, whether in software, hardware, configurations, or human factors, that could be exploited by attackers.

2) **Risk Assessment:** It assesses and categorizes the severity of vulnerabilities to prioritize mitigation efforts based on their potential impact and likelihood of exploitation.

3) **Preventing Exploitation:** By identifying vulnerabilities proactively, organizations can take steps to address and remediate these issues before they are exploited by attackers.

4) **Risk Management:** It helps organizations identify and assess security risks, allowing them to prioritize and allocate resources for remediation.

5) **Compliance:** Many industries and regulatory standards require regular vulnerability assessments and remediation as part of compliance efforts.

6) **Security Enhancement:** Vulnerability testing helps organizations proactively improve their security posture, reducing the likelihood of security breaches and data breaches.

7) **Security Awareness:** It increases awareness about potential security weaknesses among IT and security teams.

Vulnerability Testing involves several steps:

1) **Identification:** Vulnerability testing begins with the identification of potential vulnerabilities within the target system or application. This may involve using automated vulnerability scanning tools, manual testing, or a combination of both.

2) **Assessment:** After identifying vulnerabilities, they are assessed to determine their severity and potential impact on the system or application's security. Vulnerabilities are often rated based on a scale (e.g., Common Vulnerability Scoring System or CVSS) to prioritize remediation efforts.

3) **Reporting:** Vulnerabilities are documented and reported, typically including detailed information about the identified issues, their potential impact, and recommendations for mitigation or remediation.

4) **Mitigation:** Once vulnerabilities are identified, organizations can take steps to mitigate or remediate them. This may involve patching software, reconfiguring systems, implementing security measures, or other actions to reduce the risk of exploitation.

5) **Retesting:** After mitigation efforts are completed, it's common to perform retesting to confirm that the vulnerabilities have been successfully addressed.

Tools used to do Vulnerability Testing

1) Nessus
2) OpenVAS (Open Vulnerability Assessment System)
3) Nexpose (Rapid7 InsightVM):
4) Qualys
5) Burp Suite
6) Metasploit
7) Acunetix
8) Nikto
9) OWASP ZAP (Zed Attack Proxy)

Question 13. What a test Manager do?

Answer: A Test Manager is a key role within the software testing domain, responsible for overseeing and managing the testing activities within a project or an organization. The primary responsibilities and tasks of a Test Manager typically include:

1) **Test Planning:** Creating test plans and strategies for the overall testing activities, including defining the scope, objectives, resources, and timelines.

2) **Resource Management:** Assigning tasks, managing and coordinating the testing team, and ensuring efficient use of resources.

3) **Test Team Supervision:** Overseeing and guiding the testing team, providing leadership, mentorship, and support to testers.

4) **Quality Assurance:** Ensuring the quality of the testing process and the delivered software by defining quality standards and implementing best practices.

5) **Risk Management:** Identifying and mitigating risks associated with testing activities to ensure project success.

6) **Test Case Creation and Review:** Ensuring the creation and maintenance of test cases, reviewing test plans, and ensuring comprehensive test coverage.

7) **Communication:** Facilitating effective communication between the testing team, development team, stakeholders, and project managers to ensure everyone is aligned with project goals.

8) **Metrics and Reporting:** Creating and presenting test reports, metrics, and status updates to stakeholders, including defect reports and testing progress.

9) **Tool Selection and Implementation:** Identifying, evaluating, and implementing testing tools and frameworks to improve testing efficiency.

10) **Continuous Improvement:** Implementing improvements in testing methodologies, processes, and tools, and learning from past projects to enhance future testing practices.

11) **Test Environment Management:** Overseeing and managing test environments, ensuring their readiness and stability for testing.

12) **Test Automation Strategy:** Developing and implementing a strategy for test automation, overseeing the creation of automated tests and frameworks.

13) **Compliance and Standards:** Ensuring adherence to industry standards, regulatory compliance, and best practices in testing.

14) **Coordination with Project Management:** Collaborating with project managers to align testing activities with project timelines and goals.

15) **Client Interaction:** Interacting with clients or stakeholders to provide testing updates and address concerns or queries regarding testing.

Q14. Explain your latest role in Details?

Answer: Explain your role and responsibilities project wise like:

a) how many projects do you handle,
b) how many resources
c) How you manage daily tasks and reporting etc.

Question 15. How you will check the Automation script quality developed by your team?

Answer: Checking the quality of automation scripts developed by a team is crucial to ensure that the scripts are robust, maintainable, and provide accurate test coverage. Here are some key steps to check the quality of automation scripts:

1) **Code Review:** Perform thorough code reviews of the automation scripts. This involves examining the code for best practices, readability, maintainability, and adherence to coding standards.

2) **Adherence to Design Patterns:** Check if the automation scripts follow appropriate design patterns and coding principles, such as Page Object Model (POM), modular design, or other established frameworks.

3) **Test Coverage Analysis:** Ensure the automation scripts cover a wide range of test scenarios and functionalities. Analyze the code to verify that critical paths and edge cases are covered.

4) **Maintainability:** Evaluate the scripts for maintainability, ensuring that changes or updates can be made easily without significant rework.

5) **Error Handling and Reporting:** Check for proper error handling mechanisms and comprehensive reporting in the scripts to provide meaningful logs and insights when tests fail.

6) **Parameterization and Reusability:** Ensure scripts use parameterization where necessary and promote reusability of code to prevent redundancy.

7) **Performance and Efficiency:** Analyze the scripts for efficiency, looking for opportunities to optimize script execution time and resource usage.

8) **Documentation and Comments:** Assess the presence and quality of documentation and comments within the codebase to aid understanding and maintenance.

9) **Dependency Management:** Check how well the scripts manage dependencies, ensuring a clear separation of concerns and maintainability.

10) **Integration with CI/CD:** Evaluate how well the scripts integrate with Continuous Integration/Continuous Deployment (CI/CD) pipelines and their compatibility with version control systems.

11) **Regression Suitability:** Assess the scripts' suitability for regression testing, ensuring they are resilient to application changes and scalable for ongoing use.

12) **Compliance with Standards:** Ensure adherence to coding standards, naming conventions, and established best practices in automation testing.

13) **Test Execution Review:** Review the results of test executions to ensure the scripts perform as expected and provide accurate outcomes.

Question 16. What are different Test estimation Techniques?

Answer: Test estimation is a critical aspect of software testing, helping in planning and allocating resources effectively. Various techniques are used to estimate testing efforts. Some common test estimation techniques include:

1) **Expert Judgment:** In this technique, experienced individuals, including testers, team leads, or stakeholders, provide estimates based on their expertise and past experiences.

> **Applicability:** Useful when experienced individuals have a strong understanding of project requirements and the testing scope.
> **Limitation:** May be subjective and dependent on the expertise and biases of the individuals providing the estimates.

2) **Analogous Estimation:** This technique involves using historical data from similar projects to estimate the effort required for testing the current project. It relies on similarities between past and present projects to gauge effort.

> **Applicability:** Beneficial when historical data from similar projects is available and relevant to the current project.

Limitation: May not be accurate if the current project significantly differs from historical ones.

3) **Delphi Technique:** A consensus-based technique where a group of experts provides independent estimates. These estimates are then discussed, and a collective estimate is reached through multiple iterations until a consensus is achieved.

> **Applicability:** Useful when seeking unbiased estimates from a panel of experts to reach a consensus.
> **Limitation:** Time-consuming and may require multiple rounds for convergence.

4) **Three-Point Estimation (PERT):** Based on three estimates for each task: Most Likely (m), Optimistic (o), and Pessimistic (p). These estimates are then combined using the PERT formula to calculate an expected time.

> **Applicability:** Helpful when there's uncertainty in task durations, providing an average estimate based on optimistic, pessimistic, and most likely scenarios.
> **Limitation:** Assumes a specific distribution of tasks, which might not always hold true.

5) **Bottom-Up Estimation:** Estimates are made at a granular level for smaller tasks or components, and these individual estimates are aggregated to create an overall estimation for the project.

> **Applicability:** Ideal for breaking down larger tasks into smaller, manageable ones for more accurate estimation.
> **Limitation:** Can be time-consuming, especially for complex projects with numerous tasks.

6) **Parametric Estimation:** Uses historical data and statistical methods to calculate the effort required for testing based on specific project parameters and metrics.

> **Applicability:** Effective when historical data and mathematical models can provide accurate estimates based on specific project parameters and metrics.
> **Limitation:** Accuracy heavily relies on the relevance and accuracy of the data and the appropriateness of the selected parameters.

7) **Use-Case Point Analysis:** A technique used to estimate the testing effort based on the number and complexity of use cases in the software.

> **Applicability:** Suited for projects where use cases or functional points are the primary drivers of effort estimation.
> **Limitation:** Might not cover all aspects of testing and may not be suitable for non-functional testing.

8) **COCOMO (Constructive Cost Model):** An algorithmic approach that considers different factors like lines of code, cost drivers, and complexity to estimate testing effort.

> **Applicability:** Suitable for considering various factors like lines of code, cost drivers, and complexity in a project to estimate testing effort.
> **Limitation:** Complexity in application and may require experienced estimators to provide accurate inputs.

Question 17. What special you represent in your Test Report?

Answer: To make your test report stand out and provide valuable information, consider including the following special elements:

1) **Visual Representation:** Use graphs, charts, and visual aids to present test metrics, trends, and key findings. Visual representations can help stakeholders quickly grasp complex information.

2) **Risk Assessment and Mitigation:** Include a section highlighting identified risks, their potential impact, and proposed mitigation strategies. This provides stakeholders with a clear understanding of potential threats to the project.

3) **Comparative Analysis:** Consider including comparative analysis if relevant historical data is available. Show improvements or regressions in metrics and defects compared to previous testing cycles.

4) **Root Cause Analysis:** If appropriate, provide an analysis of the root causes behind critical defects or issues. Understanding the underlying causes can help in preventing similar problems in the future.

5) **Trend Analysis and Forecasting:** Use historical data to predict future trends, identify patterns, and provide forecasts for potential risks or areas that may need special attention in upcoming phases.

6) **Key Learnings and Best Practices:** Share insights gained during the testing process and highlight any best practices or lessons learned that can benefit future testing efforts.

7) **Customer Impact Analysis:** Assess how identified issues might impact end-users or customers and their overall experience. Understanding this impact can help prioritize issue resolution.

8) **Compliance and Standards Conformance:** Include a section discussing the compliance status, addressing how well the tested software aligns with industry standards, regulations, or specific compliance requirements.

9) **Cost-Benefit Analysis:** Discuss the cost implications of identified issues and the potential benefits or savings associated with resolving them.

10) **Stakeholder-Specific Insights:** Tailor sections of the report to cater to different stakeholder needs. For instance, provide more technical details for the development team and high-level summaries for management.

Question 18. What is POM approach in Automation?

Answer: The Page Object Model (POM) is a design pattern used in automated testing, particularly for web-based applications. It helps in creating a more structured and maintainable framework for testing web pages by representing each page as a separate class or object.

Question 19. Where you use the Saucelabs in your project?

Answer: Sauce Labs is a cloud-based platform that offers automated testing for web and mobile applications. It provides a Selenium-based infrastructure for running tests on various combinations of browsers, operating systems, and devices in the cloud.

Sauce Labs can be used in projects for a variety of reasons:

1) **Cross-Browser and Cross-Device Testing:** One of the primary uses of Sauce Labs is to conduct testing across different browsers (Chrome, Firefox, Safari, etc.) and devices (desktop, mobile, tablet) to ensure the application functions consistently across various environments.

2) **Parallel Testing:** Running tests in parallel on multiple browsers or devices simultaneously, which can significantly reduce test execution time.

3) **Automation Testing:**
4) Integrating with automation testing frameworks like Selenium or Appium to execute automated test scripts in the Sauce Labs cloud.

5) **Real Device Testing:** Sauce Labs offers real device testing, allowing you to test applications on actual devices instead of emulators, ensuring a more accurate representation of how the application behaves on real user devices.

6) **Continuous Integration/Continuous Deployment (CI/CD):** Integrating with CI/CD pipelines to automatically trigger tests on Sauce Labs with every build or deployment, ensuring continuous testing and quality control.

7) **Manual Testing:** Offering a platform for manual testing where testers can interact with applications on different browsers and devices manually.

8) **Debugging:** Using Sauce Labs for debugging purposes by providing videos and logs for each test run to identify issues or bugs in different environments.

9) **Scalability and Infrastructure:** Utilizing Sauce Labs' scalable infrastructure, reducing the need for maintaining an extensive in-house testing environment.

Question 20. What kind of domain knowledge do you have?

Answer:
1. Airline
2. Banking
3. Insurance
4. Hospitality
5. Education
6. E-commerce
7. AI/ML
8. HR-Tools etc.

Question 21. What is the consideration in your mind when you create a framework?

Answer: When creating a testing framework, various considerations should be taken into account to ensure its effectiveness, maintainability, and scalability. Some key considerations include:

1) **Scope and Objectives:** Define the framework's purpose, including the types of tests it will support, the technologies it will be used with, and the intended scope of its application.

2) **Technology Stack:** Choose the appropriate tools, libraries, and programming languages based on the application under test and the team's expertise. For instance, selecting Selenium for web automation or Appium for mobile automation.

3) **Modularity and Reusability:** Design the framework to be modular, allowing for easy reuse of components (functions, methods, test cases) across different tests. Implement design patterns like Page Object Model (POM) for maintainability.

4) **Scalability and Maintainability:** Create a framework that is scalable and easily maintainable, ensuring it can accommodate the growth of the application and changes in requirements over time. Minimize redundancy and maximize code reusability.

5) **Test Data Management:** Determine how test data will be managed, whether it's through external files, databases, or any other means. Separate test data from test scripts for easy maintenance.

6) **Reporting and Logging:** Implement robust reporting and logging mechanisms to provide detailed test execution reports and logs. Consider integration with Continuous Integration (CI) tools for enhanced reporting.

7) **Configuration Management:** Manage configurations for different environments (dev, test, staging, production) to ensure seamless testing across various setups.

8) **Integration and Extensibility:** Plan for integration with other tools, frameworks, or CI/CD pipelines to achieve automation throughout the software development lifecycle. Make the framework extensible for future integrations.

9) **Error Handling and Recovery Scenarios:** Design the framework to handle exceptions and errors gracefully, with predefined recovery scenarios to continue test execution whenever possible.

10) **Test Execution Speed and Parallel Execution:** Optimize the framework to run tests quickly by implementing parallel execution, reducing the overall test execution time.

11) **Community Support and Best Practices:** Leverage best practices, standards, and community support for the chosen tools and frameworks. Utilize resources like forums, documentation, and user communities for guidance.

12) **Cross-Browser and Cross-Device Testing:** If applicable, consider how the framework will support testing on various browsers and devices. Integration with cloud-based testing services like Sauce Labs can be beneficial.

13) **Training and Support:** Consider the training and support needed for the testing team to effectively use the framework.

14) **Version Control:** Use version control systems (e.g., Git) to manage the framework code, allowing for collaborative development and tracking changes.

15) **Community and Best Practices:** Leverage industry best practices and learn from the testing community's experiences to build a robust and efficient framework.

16) **Documentation:** Thoroughly document the framework, including guidelines for writing test scripts, configuring the framework, and troubleshooting common issues

Question 22. What are the main limitations to choose the Selenium automation Framework?

Answer: Selenium is a popular and powerful tool for automated web application testing. However, like any technology or framework, it also has its limitations. Some of the main limitations of choosing the Selenium automation framework include:

1) **Limited Support for Desktop Applications:** Selenium primarily focuses on web application testing and doesn't offer comprehensive support for testing desktop applications or mobile apps (except through Selenium-Appium for mobile apps).

2) **No Built-in Reporting or Logging:** Selenium lacks built-in reporting and logging functionalities. While there are third-party tools and frameworks that can be integrated, Selenium itself does not provide native support for comprehensive reporting and logging.

3) **Challenges with Handling Dynamic Elements:** Dynamically changing web elements or elements within i-frames can pose challenges. Selenium may encounter issues identifying or interacting with such elements, leading to test failures.

4) **Cross-Domain Security Restrictions:** Selenium has limitations when dealing with cross-domain security restrictions, which can impact its ability to automate testing in situations involving i-frames or cross-domain interactions.

5) **Complexity with Non-HTML Elements:** Selenium struggles with handling non-HTML elements like PDFs, images, or CAPTCHA, making it less effective in automating testing for these types of components.

6) **Maintenance Effort:** Test scripts in Selenium frameworks can be sensitive to changes in the application's structure. Test maintenance can be labor-intensive, especially when there are frequent UI updates or changes in the application.

7) **Learning Curve:** For beginners or those without a programming background, Selenium may have a steep learning curve. Writing effective and efficient test scripts often requires a good understanding of programming languages and concepts.

8) **Limited Support for Image-Based Testing:** Selenium primarily focuses on element-based interaction. It lacks robust native support for image-based testing.

9) **Scalability with Large Test Suites:** As test suites grow larger, managing and scaling Selenium-based tests can become complex, potentially leading to increased maintenance effort and longer execution times.

Question 23. What are the different types of assertions you use in your framework?

Answer: Hard Assertions and Soft Assertions

There are several types of assertions that can be used to verify expected outcomes in web applications:

1) assertEqual: This assertion checks if two values are equal.
2) assertNotEqual: This assertion checks if two values are not equal.

3) assertTrue: This assertion checks if a condition is true.
4) assertFalse: This assertion checks if a condition is false.
5) assertIn: This assertion checks if a value is present in a list or a string.
6) assertNotIn: This assertion checks if a value is not present in a list or a string.
7) assertIs: This assertion checks if two objects are the same object.
8) assertIsNot: This assertion checks if two objects are not the same object.
9) assertIsNone: This assertion checks if a value is None.
10) assertIsNotNone: This assertion checks if a value is not None.
11) assertAlmostEqual: This assertion checks if two values are almost equal.
12) assertNotAlmostEqual: This assertion checks if two values are not almost equal.

Question 24. What type of error do you get when assertions get fail?

Answer: When an assertion fails, an AssertionError is raised, and the test execution stops. The error message associated with the AssertionError will typically provide information about the specific assertion that failed, including the line number and file where the assertion occurred, as well as any relevant context or details about the failed assertion.

For example, if you have a test case that checks if a button is enabled after performing a certain action, and the button is not enabled, the assertion will fail, and an AssertionError will be raised with a message indicating that the button is not enabled as expected.

It is important to handle these errors appropriately by either fixing the issue that caused the assertion to fail or updating the assertion to reflect the expected behavior of the web application. Proper handling of these errors will help in identifying and resolving issues in the web application and improving the overall quality of the software.

Question 25. Explain where you use encapsulation and polymorphism in your project.

Answer: Encapsulation is an important concept in object-oriented programming that can be applied in Selenium automation projects to improve code organization, flexibility, and maintainability. In Selenium automation, encapsulation can be used to create classes that represent web pages or components, and expose methods to interact with them.

For example, you can create a class representing a login page, and encapsulate the methods that interact with the login form elements within that class. These methods may include filling out the username and password fields, clicking the login button, and verifying that the user has been successfully logged in.

By encapsulating these methods within a login page class, other parts of the code can interact with the login page through its public interface, without needing to know the details of how the login page is implemented. This makes the code more modular and easier to maintain, as changes to the implementation of the login page can be made without affecting other parts of the code.

Similarly, you can create classes representing other web pages or components, such as a registration page, a search results page, or a navigation bar. By encapsulating the methods that interact with these pages or components within their respective classes, you can create a more organized and maintainable Selenium automation project.

Overall, encapsulation is a powerful tool for creating well-organized and modular Selenium automation projects, by hiding the implementation details of individual pages or components behind a public interface that other parts of the code can interact with.

Question 26. What are the different design patterns that you use in your automation framework?

Question 27. What is Static in Java? Explain at least 7 points about it?

Answer: In Java, the keyword static is used to create variables, methods, and nested classes that belong to a class rather than to an instance of the class. Here are seven key points about static in Java:

1. **Static variables:** A static variable is a class-level variable that is shared by all instances of the class. It can be accessed using the class name, without creating an object of the class.

2. **Static methods:** A static method is a class-level method that can be called without creating an object of the class. It can only access static variables and other static methods of the class.

3. **Static blocks:** A static block is a block of code that is executed when the class is loaded into memory. It is used to initialize static variables or perform other class-level operations.

4. **Static nested classes:** A static nested class is a class that is declared inside another class, but does not have access to the instance variables or methods of the outer class. It can be instantiated without creating an object of the outer class.

5. **Constants:** Constants can be defined as static final variables, which means that they cannot be modified after they are initialized, and are shared by all instances of the class.

6. **Memory allocation:** Static variables and methods are allocated memory in the class area of the JVM, rather than in the heap area where objects are stored.

7. **Utility methods:** Static methods are often used to define utility methods, which perform common operations that do not require access to instance variables. These methods can be called without creating an object of the class, which can make the code more concise and efficient.

Overall, static is a powerful concept in Java that allows you to create class-level variables, methods, and nested classes, which can be shared by all instances of the class, and do not require an object of the class to be created. This can lead to more efficient and concise code, and is particularly useful for defining utility methods and constants.

Question 28. How do you use a simple text file and JSON file in your project?
Answer: In a Java automation project, you can use text files and JSON files in much the same way as in a Python project. Here are some examples of how you might use these file types in a Java automation project:

1.Reading a JSON file:

import java.io.FileReader;

```java
import com.google.gson.JsonObject;
import com.google.gson.JsonParser;

// Open the JSON file and load the data
JsonObject configData = null;
try (FileReader reader = new FileReader("config.json")) {
    JsonParser parser = new JsonParser();
    configData = parser.parse(reader).getAsJsonObject();
}

// Use the data as needed
String apiKey = configData.get("api_key").getAsString();
String baseUrl = configData.get("base_url").getAsString();
```

2.Writing a text file

```java
import java.io.FileWriter;
import java.io.IOException;

// Open the file for writing
try (FileWriter writer = new FileWriter("output.txt")) {
    // Write some data to the file
    writer.write("Here is some output data\n");
    writer.write("And some more data\n");
} catch (IOException e) {
    // Handle the exception
}
```

3.Reading a text file:

```java
import java.io.FileReader;
import java.io.IOException;
import java.io.BufferedReader;

// Open the file for reading
try (BufferedReader reader = new BufferedReader(new FileReader("input.txt"))) {
    // Read the contents of the file
    String inputLine;
    StringBuilder inputText = new StringBuilder();
    while ((inputLine = reader.readLine()) != null) {
        inputText.append(inputLine);
    }

    // Use the input data as needed
    String[] urls = inputText.toString().split("\\n");
} catch (IOException e) {
    // Handle the exception
}
```

Question 29. What are the different components of a Header in any request?

Answer: In a request message, the header contains metadata about the request, including information about the client making the request, the server receiving the request, and the message body being sent or received. Here are the different components of the header in any request:

1. **Request line:** The first line of the header contains the HTTP method being used (such as GET or POST), the resource being requested (such as a URL or file path), and the HTTP version being used
2. **Request headers:** These are additional fields in the header that provide metadata about the request, including information about the client, the message body, and any custom headers that may be included. Some common request headers include:
   a) Host: The domain name or IP address of the server receiving the request.
   b) User-Agent: Information about the client making the request, such as the web browser or application being used.
   c) Accept: The format of the data the client is willing to accept in the response.
   d) Content-Type: The format of the data being sent in the request.
   e) Authorization: Credentials for accessing a protected resource, such as a username and password or an access token.
   f) Cache-Control: Instructions for caching the response, such as how long the response should be cached.
3. **Empty line:** A blank line that separates the header from the message body.
4. **Message body:** This is the data being sent in the request, if any. The message body is optional, and not all requests will include one.

Question 30. Who assigned test cases to your team, you, or your test leads?

Answer: Test Lead

Question 31. How do you measure the cost of quality?

Answer: As a test manager, measuring the cost of quality involves identifying and quantifying the costs associated with ensuring that a product or service meets or exceeds customer expectations. Some methods include:

1) **Failure costs:** Identify the costs of defects or nonconformance, including costs for rework, repairs, and warranty claims. This can be done by keeping track of the number of defects found and their severity, and the cost to fix them.

2) **Prevention costs:** Identify the costs associated with preventing defects or nonconformance, including costs for quality planning, inspection, and testing. This can be done by keeping track of the time and resources spent on test planning, test design and test execution.

3) **Appraisal costs:** Identify the costs associated with evaluating the quality of a product or service, including costs for inspections, audits, and testing. This can be done by keeping track of the time and resources spent on test execution, test execution, and test reporting.

4) **Internal failure costs:** Identify the costs associated with defects or nonconformance that are identified and corrected before the product or service is delivered to the customer.

5) **External failure costs:** Identify the costs associated with defects or nonconformance that are identified and corrected after the product or service is delivered to the customer.

6) **Compliance costs:** Identify the costs associated with meeting regulatory and industry standards for quality, including costs for documentation, testing, and certification.

7) **Root cause analysis:** Investigate and analyse defects found to determine the root cause and identify areas where the team can improve, this can help identify the cost of quality.

8) **Statistical process control:** Use statistical techniques to monitor and control the quality of a product or service, this can help identify the cost of quality.

9) **Benchmarking:** Compare costs of quality to industry standards or to similar organizations, this can help identify areas where cost savings can be made and to measure improvement over time.

Question 32. What are the main tasks of Test Closure Activities?

Answer: Test Closure activities are the final step of the testing process and involve completing all the necessary tasks to formally conclude the testing process and close the project.
The main tasks of Test Closure activities include:

1) **Completing all test execution activities:** Ensure that all test cases have been executed, and any defects found have been addressed.

2) **Finalizing test deliverables**: Prepare and distribute final test deliverables such as test reports, test summary reports, and test closure reports.

3) **Reviewing test closure documents**: Review test closure documents such as test plans, test cases, test scripts, and test data to ensure that they are accurate and complete.

4) **Performing a lesson learned**: Perform a lesson learned analysis to identify what worked well and what didn't, to improve future testing processes.

5) **Archiving test artifacts**: Archive all test artifacts such as test cases, test scripts, test data, test results, and other documentation for future reference.

6) **Return of test environment**: Return the test environment to the original state or to the next phase of the project.

7) **Closing of defects:** Close all defects that have been resolved or deferred.

8) **Closing of open issues**: Close all open issues related to testing.

9) **Performing post-implementation review**: Perform a post-implementation review to ensure that the system has been deployed correctly and is functioning as expected.

10) **Communicating the status**: Communicate the status of the testing process and the outcome of the testing to the relevant stakeholders and project team members.

Question 33. What is Project Risk, what are some of the common project risks?

Answer: Project risk from a testing perspective refers to the potential for unforeseen events or circumstances that could negatively impact the successful completion of the testing phase of a project. Some common project risks for testing include:

1) **Schedule risk:** The potential for delays in completing the testing phase on time, due to factors such as unplanned events, resource constraints, or changes in project scope.
2) **Quality risk:** The potential for defects or nonconformance in the product or service being tested, which could lead to customer dissatisfaction or increased costs for rework, repairs, or warranty claims.
3) **Testing resource risk:** The potential for a lack of skilled or experienced testing resources, which could lead to delays or increased costs for the testing phase.

4) **Test data risk:** The potential for missing or incorrect test data, which could lead to defects or nonconformance in the product or service being tested.

5) **Test environment risk:** The potential for issues with the test environment, such as lack of access or compatibility issues, which could lead to delays or increased costs for the testing phase.

6) **Test automation risk:** The potential for issues with test automation tools, such as defects in the automation scripts, which could lead to delays or increased costs for the testing phase.

7) **System integration risk:** The potential for issues with integrating the system with other systems, which could lead to defects or nonconformance in the product or service being tested.

8) **Third-party software risk:** The potential for issues with third-party software, such as compatibility issues or lack of support, which could lead to defects or nonconformance in the product or service being tested.

9) **Test coverage risk:** The potential for not having enough test coverage, which could lead to defects or nonconformance in the product or service being tested.

10) **Test maintenance risk:** The potential for issues with maintaining and updating test cases, which could lead to defects or nonconformance in the product or service being tested

Question 34. How you generate test logs in automation testing framework?

Answer: Maven is a build automation tool and does not directly influence how logs are generated during test execution. The choice of logging framework depends on your programming language, and popular ones include Log4j, SLF4J with Logback, or the built-in logging module in languages like Python.

Here's a general guide on how you can generate test logs in a Maven-based automation testing framework:

1. Add Logging Dependencies to Maven POM:

For example, if you are using Log4j in a Java project, add the following dependencies to your Maven POM file:

```
<dependencies>
  <!-- Log4j dependencies -->
  <dependency>
    <groupId>org.apache.logging.log4j</groupId>
    <artifactId>log4j-api</artifactId>
    <version>2.14.1</version>
  </dependency>
```

```xml
    <dependency>
      <groupId>org.apache.logging.log4j</groupId>
      <artifactId>log4j-core</artifactId>
      <version>2.14.1</version>
    </dependency>
  </dependencies>
```

2. Configure Logging:

Create a log configuration file (e.g., log4j2.xml for Log4j) to configure the logging behavior. Place this file in the src/test/resources directory.

```xml
<!-- log4j2.xml -->
<Configuration>
  <Appenders>
    <Console name="Console" target="SYSTEM_OUT">
      <PatternLayout pattern="%d{HH:mm:ss.SSS} [%t] %-5level %logger{36} - %msg%n"/>
    </Console>
  </Appenders>
  <Loggers>
    <Root level="info">
      <AppenderRef ref="Console"/>
    </Root>
  </Loggers>
</Configuration>
```

3. Initialize Logging in Test Code:
In your test code, initialize the logging system at the beginning of your test suite or test execution.

```java
import org.apache.logging.log4j.LogManager;
import org.apache.logging.log4j.Logger;

public class YourTestClass {

    private static final Logger logger = LogManager.getLogger(YourTestClass.class);

    @Test
    public void yourTestMethod() {
        // Example log statements
        logger.info("This is an informational message");
        logger.warn("This is a warning message");
        logger.error("This is an error message");
    }
}
```

4. Run Tests with Maven:
Execute your tests using Maven commands. Maven will use the dependencies specified in your POM file to manage the classpath, including the logging framework.

mvn clean test

5. View Logs:

Logs will be generated according to the configuration specified in your log configuration file. You can view logs in the console or log files, depending on your configuration.

This example is specific to Log4j, but the general approach is similar for other logging frameworks. Adjust the dependencies, configuration files, and initialization code based on your chosen logging framework and language.

Question 35. Is it a good idea to have two types of logging mechanisms in an automation testing framework?

Answer: Having two types of logging mechanisms in an automation testing framework can be justified in certain scenarios, depending on the requirements and goals of your testing project. However, it's essential to carefully evaluate the need for multiple logging mechanisms and ensure that they serve distinct purposes without causing unnecessary complexity. Here are some considerations:

Reasons to Have Multiple Logging Mechanisms:

1. **Dual-Purpose Logs:**
   You may use one logging mechanism for general purpose logs that capture high-level information, test progress, and critical errors for immediate feedback during test execution. Another logging mechanism can be designed for detailed debugging information, including variable values, stack traces, and low-level details. These logs are typically used during troubleshooting and debugging phases.

2. **Integration with External Systems:**
   If your project requires integration with external monitoring or logging systems that have specific format or structure requirements, you might use one logging mechanism for internal use and another for external integration.

3. **Legacy Systems or Dependencies:**
   In some cases, a legacy system or dependency might require a specific logging mechanism. You might need to maintain compatibility with such systems while using a more modern and versatile logging framework for the rest of the automation framework.

4. **Team Preferences or Standards:**
   Different teams or team members might have preferences for different logging frameworks or mechanisms. If it doesn't introduce significant complexity, allowing some flexibility in logging tools could be a compromise.

Question 36. What are the different ways by which create jobs on Jenkins?

Answer: Jenkins provides various ways to create jobs, allowing flexibility for different types of projects and configurations. Here are different methods to create jobs on Jenkins:

Freestyle Project:

Description: A freestyle project is the simplest and most common type of Jenkins job. It allows you to configure build steps, post-build actions, and other parameters through a web-based interface.

How to Create:
a) Go to the Jenkins dashboard.
b) Click on "New Item."
c) Enter a name for your project, choose "Freestyle project," and click "OK."

d) Configure build steps, post-build actions, and other settings as needed.

Pipeline:

Description: Jenkins Pipeline is a suite of plugins that allows you to define an entire build, test, and deployment pipeline as code. It supports both Declarative and Scripted Pipeline syntax.

How to Create:

1. Go to the Jenkins dashboard.
2. Click on "New Item."
3. Enter a name for your project, choose "Pipeline," and click "OK."
4. Configure the pipeline using either Declarative or Scripted syntax in the Pipeline script section.

Multibranch Pipeline:

Description: A Multibranch Pipeline allows Jenkins to automatically discover, manage, and run branches of your project. It is useful for projects hosted on version control systems like Git.

How to Create:

a) Go to the Jenkins dashboard.
b) Click on "New Item."
c) Enter a name for your project, choose "Multibranch Pipeline," and click "OK."
d) Configure the branch source (e.g., Git) and other settings.

GitHub Organization:

Description: The GitHub Organization job type automatically creates Jenkins jobs for repositories in a GitHub organization. It's a convenient way to set up Jenkins jobs for multiple projects in a GitHub organization.

How to Create:

a) Go to the Jenkins dashboard.
b) Click on "New Item."
c) Enter a name for your project, choose "GitHub Organization," and click "OK."
d) Configure GitHub organization details and credentials.

Job DSL:

Description: Job DSL (Domain Specific Language) is a plugin that allows you to define Jenkins jobs using a Groovy-based DSL. It's useful for creating jobs programmatically and managing them as code.

How to Create:

a) Install the Job DSL plugin in Jenkins.
b) Create a new Freestyle project.
c) Add a build step using the "Process Job DSLs" option.
d) Write your Job DSL script to define jobs.

Copy Existing Job:

Description: You can duplicate an existing job as a template for new jobs. This is useful when you have similar configurations for multiple projects.

How to Create:

a) Go to the Jenkins dashboard.
b) Locate the existing job you want to copy.
c) Click on "Copy" or "New Copy" in the job's options.
d) Modify the copied job as needed.

Question 37. What are the stages to build Jenkins pipeline for automation testing project?

Answer: Building a Jenkins pipeline for an automation testing project involves defining stages that encompass the various steps of your testing workflow. Below are typical stages you might include in a Jenkins pipeline for an automation testing project:

1. Initialization:
Description: Set up the initial environment, clone the repository, and install any dependencies required for testing.

2. Static Code Analysis (Optional):
Description: Run static code analysis tools to identify potential issues in the test code.

3. Unit Testing:
Description: Execute unit tests to verify the correctness of individual units or components.

4.Integration Testing:
Description: Conduct integration tests to validate the interactions between components or systems.

5. Code Coverage (Optional):
Description: Measure code coverage to assess how much of your codebase is exercised by your tests.

6. Artifact Archiving (Optional):
Description: Archive test artifacts for later analysis or reporting.

7. Security Scanning (Optional):
Description: Perform security scanning to identify vulnerabilities in dependencies or code.

8. Deployment (Optional):
Description: If applicable, deploy the tested application to a staging environment for further testing.

9. Report Generation:
Description: Generate test reports to provide insights into test results.

10. Notification:
Description: Notify relevant stakeholders about the status of the test execution.

11. Post-Build Cleanup (Optional):
Description: Perform any necessary cleanup tasks after the testing stages, such as releasing resources or cleaning up temporary files.

12. Finalization:

Description: Perform any finalization steps, such as archiving artifacts or triggering additional actions.

These stages provide a basic structure for a Jenkins pipeline in an automation testing project. Customize the pipeline stages based on your specific testing requirements and workflow. Additionally, you may include additional stages or steps depending on the complexity of your testing process.

Question 38. What are pre-sales activities for a Test Manager?

Pre-sales activities for a Test Manager involve tasks and responsibilities that contribute to the pre-contract phase, usually before a project or service is sold to a client. These activities are essential to ensure that the testing aspect of the project is well understood, planned, and communicated effectively.

Here are some pre-sales activities for a Test Manager:

1. **Understanding Client Requirements:**
   a) Collaborate with sales and business development teams to gather information about the client's testing requirements and objectives.
   b) Conduct meetings with potential clients to understand their testing needs, project goals, and constraints.

2. **Proposal Development:**
   a) Assist in preparing proposals and bids for potential testing projects. This includes estimating project costs, timelines, and resource requirements.
   b) Create detailed testing project plans that outline the scope, objectives, deliverables, and testing methodologies.

3. **Risk Assessment:**
   a) Identify and assess potential risks and challenges associated with the testing project.
   b) Develop risk mitigation strategies and contingency plans to address potential issues.

4. **Solution Design:**
   a) Work with technical experts and QA teams to design testing solutions that align with the client's needs and project goals.
   b) Define the testing strategy, including the selection of testing tools, frameworks, and methodologies.

5. **Cost Estimation:**
   a) Develop a budget for the testing project, considering factors like resource costs, tool licenses, and other expenses.
   b) Ensure that the proposed budget is competitive and aligned with the client's expectations.

6. **Client Communication:**
   a) Maintain effective communication with the client throughout the presales process.
   b) Address client inquiries, concerns, and provide clarifications as needed.

7. **Presentation and Demonstrations:**
   a) Prepare and deliver presentations or product demonstrations to showcase the capabilities and expertise of the testing team.
   b) Highlight the value proposition of your testing services and how they can meet the client's specific needs.

8. **Tailoring Testing Solutions:**
   a) Customize testing solutions to meet the unique requirements and constraints of the client's industry and project.

b) Highlight the benefits and advantages of your tailored approach.

9. **Case Studies and References:**
   a) Share relevant case studies and references of past successful testing projects to build trust and confidence with potential clients.

10. **Competitive Analysis:**
    a) Analyze the competition and identify the unique selling points (USPs) of your testing services.
    b) Showcase how your team can provide better value or differentiation.

11. **Legal and Compliance:**
    a) Collaborate with legal and compliance teams to ensure that contracts, agreements, and terms and conditions meet both the client's and your organization's requirements.

12. **Handover to Project Management:**

Once a project is won, ensure a smooth transition to the project management team, providing them with all necessary information and insights gathered during the presales phase.

Question 39. Describe your experience with test planning and test case design?

Answer: Test planning and test case design are critical components of ensuring the quality of the software being developed. Here's an overview of my experience and approach in these areas:

Test Planning:

a) Understanding Requirements: I work closely with project stakeholders to understand project requirements, user stories, and functional specifications. Clear comprehension of the project objectives is essential for effective test planning.

b) Risk Assessment: I conduct a risk analysis to identify potential areas of risk within the project, considering aspects such as critical functionalities, dependencies, and potential bottlenecks. This helps prioritize testing efforts.

c) Resource Allocation: I allocate human and technical resources effectively. This involves assigning tasks, defining roles, and ensuring the necessary tools and infrastructure are available to execute testing.

d) Test Strategy Development: I create a comprehensive test strategy that outlines the testing approach, test levels, and types to be employed. This strategy serves as a roadmap for the testing process.

e) Documentation: I ensure that the test plan document is well-documented, detailing the scope, objectives, entry/exit criteria, resources, schedules, and metrics to measure progress and success.

Test Case Design:

a) Requirement Traceability: I emphasize traceability by mapping test cases to specific requirements. Each test case is tied to a particular feature, ensuring comprehensive coverage of the software's functionality.

b) Clear and Concise Test Cases: I promote the creation of clear, concise, and understandable test cases. Each test case includes a description, preconditions, steps to reproduce, expected outcomes, and actual outcomes once executed.

c) Prioritization and Optimization: I prioritize test cases based on risk, criticality, and impact. Not all test cases are equally important, so I focus on high-priority scenarios first to ensure critical aspects are thoroughly tested.

d) Reusable Test Design: I encourage the creation of reusable test components to optimize efficiency. Test cases that can be used across different scenarios or functionalities help reduce redundancy and save time.

e) Continuous Improvement: I foster an environment of continuous improvement, regularly reviewing and updating test cases to reflect changes in requirements, technology, or lessons learned from testing.

Question 40. How will you build QA practice as a Test professional?

Answer: Building a successful QA (Quality Assurance) practice as a **Test professional** involves several strategic and practical steps. Here's a comprehensive guide to help you establish an effective QA practice:

1. Understand the Project:
   a) Gain a deep understanding of the project's goals, requirements, and objectives.
   b) Identify key stakeholders and their expectations.
   c) Determine the critical quality attributes and success criteria for the project.

2. Define QA Strategy:
   a) Create a QA strategy that aligns with the project's goals and objectives.
   b) Determine the testing methodologies (e.g., manual, automated, performance, security) that will be employed.
   c) Define the scope of testing and identify the testing environments.
   d) Set clear expectations for defect management, reporting, and communication.

3. Build a Skilled QA Team:
   a) Recruit and hire skilled QA engineers and testers based on project needs.
   b) Provide training and skill development opportunities to enhance the team's expertise.
   c) Foster a culture of collaboration, learning, and knowledge sharing within the QA team.

4. Develop Test Plans:
   a) Create detailed test plans outlining testing scope, objectives, resources, and timelines.
   b) Define test cases and scenarios that cover various aspects of the application.
   c) Determine entry and exit criteria for each testing phase.

5. Implement Test Processes:
   a) Establish clear testing processes and methodologies.
   b) Define how requirements will be reviewed and transformed into testable scenarios.
   c) Determine the criteria for test case creation, execution, and result analysis.

6. Test Automation:
   a) Evaluate the feasibility of test automation and identify suitable automation tools.
   b) Develop an automation strategy for repetitive and regression testing.
   c) Implement automated test scripts and maintain the automation framework.

7. **Test Execution and Reporting:**
   a) Coordinate and manage test execution activities.
   b) Monitor test progress and report on testing status, including defect metrics and test coverage.
   c) Ensure that testing aligns with the project schedule and milestones.
8. **Report and Track Defects:**
   a) Implement a robust defect tracking system that allows your team to report, prioritize, and manage defects effectively. Clear documentation of defects is crucial for the development team to understand and fix issues.
9. **Measure and Communicate QA Metrics:**
   a) Define relevant QA metrics that track the effectiveness of your testing efforts. Regularly communicate these metrics to stakeholders to demonstrate the value of QA.

10. **Continuous Improvement:**
    a) Conduct regular retrospectives to identify areas for improvement in the QA process.
    b) Encourage feedback from the QA team and stakeholders to refine processes.
    c) Implement changes based on lessons learned and best practices.

11. **Collaboration and Communication:**
    a) Foster open communication between development, QA, and other project stakeholders.
    b) Collaborate with development teams to address issues and prioritize fixes.
    c) Provide clear and concise reporting to management and stakeholders.

12. **Quality Advocacy:**
    a) Be an advocate for quality within the organization.
    b) Influence decision-making processes to prioritize quality and testing efforts.
    c) Educate stakeholders on the value of QA and the role it plays in delivering a successful project.

14. **Stay Updated:**
    a) Keep up with industry trends, emerging technologies, and best practices in QA and testing.
    b) Incorporate relevant advancements into your QA practice to stay competitive.

1. **Adapt to Change:**
   a) Be flexible and adaptive to changes in project scope, requirements, and timelines. Adjust your QA strategy as needed to accommodate these changes.
2. **Promote Quality Culture:**
   a) Encourage a culture of quality throughout the organization. QA is not just a phase; it's a mindset that should be embraced by everyone involved in the project.

Remember that building a strong QA practice is an ongoing effort that requires adaptability, continuous learning, and a commitment to quality. Customizing these steps to your organization's specific needs and culture will greatly contribute to the success of your QA

Question 41. How do you measure the success of your testing practice?

Answer: Measuring the success of your testing practices involves assessing various factors that contribute to the quality and reliability of your software. Here are some key metrics and indicators to consider when measuring the success of your testing practice:

1) **Defect Density:** Measure the number of defects found per unit of code. A decreasing defect density over time indicates improved testing effectiveness.

2) **Test Coverage:** Assess how much of your code is covered by tests. This includes both code paths and functionality covered by tests. Higher coverage suggests better testing thoroughness.

3) **Regression Rate:** Calculate the rate at which new defects are introduced in existing functionality after changes. A low regression rate indicates that new code changes aren't causing unintended side effects.

4) **Time-to-Fix:** Measure the time taken to fix defects identified during testing. A shorter time-to-fix indicates efficient defect resolution.

5) **Bug Escape Rate:** Monitor the number of defects that escape the testing phase and are identified by users after deployment. A low bug escape rate suggests effective testing at identifying issues before they reach users.

6) **Test Execution Time:** Measure how long it takes to execute your test suite. Faster test execution improves the feedback loop and overall development speed.

7) **Testing Costs:** Analyze the costs associated with testing, including tools, resources, and time. A reasonable balance between costs and quality is important.

8) **Test Case Effectiveness:** Assess the effectiveness of your test cases by tracking the ratio of passed tests to total tests executed. This helps identify areas where tests need improvement.

9) **Customer Satisfaction:** Gather feedback from users or stakeholders about the quality and performance of the software. High customer satisfaction indicates successful testing practices.

10) **Number of Production Incidents:** Monitor the number of incidents reported by users after deployment. A decrease in the number of incidents suggests improved software quality.

11) **Release Confidence:** Gauge the confidence of the development team and stakeholders in the quality of the software before each release. High confidence indicates effective testing.

12) **Code Churn Impact:** Measure the impact of frequent code changes on the stability of the software. Effective testing should mitigate the negative effects of code churn.

13) **Automated vs. Manual Tests Ratio:** Track the proportion of automated tests to manual tests. An appropriate balance indicates efficiency in both testing types.

14) **Time Spent on Regression Testing:** Measure the time spent on regression testing before each release. Optimizing regression testing time while maintaining quality is a sign of efficiency.

15) **Adherence to Schedule:** Evaluate whether testing is completed within the planned time frame. Staying on schedule indicates effective planning and execution.

16) **Metrics Improvement Over Time:** Compare your testing metrics over different testing cycles. Consistent improvement over time signifies an evolving and effective testing practice.

17) **Defect Root Cause Analysis:** Analyze the root causes of defects found during testing. Identifying and addressing the underlying issues leads to more effective testing.

18) **Testing Process Efficiency:** Continuously assess the efficiency of your testing processes by analyzing bottlenecks, unnecessary steps, and areas for improvement.

Question 42. How do you handle situations where the testing uncovers critical defects or issues that need to be resolved urgently?

Answer: Handling situations where critical defects or urgent issues are uncovered during testing requires a well-organized and proactive approach to ensure quick resolution. Here's how I would manage such scenarios:

1) **Immediate Notification:** As soon as a critical defect is identified, I would notify relevant stakeholders, including developers, project managers, and key decision-makers. Transparent communication is essential to ensure everyone is aware of the issue.

2) **Severity Assessment:** I would work with the testing team to assess the severity of the defect. This involves understanding the impact on the application's functionality, user experience, security, and overall stability.

3) **solation and Reproduction:** To provide developers with clear information, I would help isolate and reproduce the defect in a controlled environment. This includes documenting the exact steps to reproduce the issue, any specific configurations, and screenshots or videos if applicable.

4) **Bug Report:** I would ensure a detailed bug report is created and documented in your chosen bug tracking or project management system. The report would include information about the defect, its impact, steps to reproduce, and any relevant logs or error messages.

5) **Escalation:** If the critical defect requires immediate attention, I would escalate it to the development team lead or project manager. This ensures that the highest priority is assigned to resolving the issue swiftly.

6) **Collaboration with Developers:** I would collaborate closely with the development team to provide them with all necessary information about the defect. Clear and open communication helps developers understand the issue's context and aids in efficient resolution.

7) **Temporary Workarounds:** Depending on the severity of the defect and the timeline for a fix, I would work with the team to identify and implement temporary workarounds to minimize the impact on users.

8) **Regression Testing:** After the defect is resolved, I would coordinate regression testing to ensure that the fix hasn't introduced any new issues. This ensures the application remains stable and reliable.

9) **Priority Reassessment:** I would reassess the testing priorities and schedule, making adjustments if necessary to accommodate the urgency of resolving the critical issue.

10) **Post-Mortem Analysis:** After the issue is resolved, I would conduct a post-mortem analysis with the testing and development teams to identify the root cause, discuss preventive measures, and learn from the experience to improve future testing efforts.

11) **Communication with Stakeholders:** Throughout the process, I would maintain ongoing communication with stakeholders, providing updates on the issue's resolution and its impact on the project timeline.

12) **Documentation and Learning:** I would ensure that all steps taken to address the critical issue are documented for future reference. The experience gained from handling the issue contributes to continuous improvement in testing practices.

Question 43. How do you convince the difficult client as a Test Manager?

Answer: Convincing a difficult client as a test manager requires a combination of effective communication, demonstrating value, and building trust. Here's a step-by-step approach you can follow:

1) **Understand Their Concerns:** Start by actively listening to the client's concerns, requirements, and expectations. Understand what specifically is making them difficult to work with. This shows that you respect their perspective and are genuinely interested in addressing their issues.

2) **Empathize:** Show empathy towards their concerns. Acknowledge any frustrations they might be experiencing and express your understanding of their situation. This helps in building a rapport and showing that you're on their side.

3) **Clear Communication:** Clearly and transparently explain your approach to testing, the value it brings to the project, and how it aligns with their goals. Use non-technical language to avoid confusion and ensure they understand the benefits of your testing efforts.

4) **Highlight Benefits:** Emphasize the benefits of thorough testing, such as reducing the risk of defects in production, improving the user experience, and ultimately saving time and money in the long run. Use examples from previous projects where testing made a significant positive impact.

5) **Customized Solutions:** Tailor your testing approach to their specific needs and priorities. Address any concerns they have and show how your testing strategy will address those concerns directly. Offer solutions that meet their needs and address their concerns

6) **Provide Evidence:** Present data, metrics, and case studies that support your testing methodologies. Show how your approach has worked effectively in similar situations in the past.

7) **Collaborative Approach:** Position yourself as a collaborator rather than an opponent. Let them know that you're there to work together towards the success of the project and that their input is valued.

8) **Regular Updates:** Keep them informed about the progress of testing, any issues discovered, and how those issues are being addressed. Regular communication helps build trust and transparency.

9) **Mitigate Risks:** Explain how your testing efforts will identify and mitigate potential risks that could impact the project's success. This demonstrates your proactive approach to ensuring the quality of the end product.

10) **Flexibility:** Be open to their suggestions and feedback. If they have specific concerns about your testing methods, be willing to adjust and find a compromise that satisfies both parties.

11) **Conflict Resolution:** If disagreements arise, handle them professionally and calmly. Focus on finding solutions that address their concerns while still maintaining the integrity of your testing process.

12) **Showcase Progress:** Once you start finding and addressing defects through testing, share these results with them. This demonstrates the concrete value of your work and reinforces their confidence in your abilities.

13) **Continuous Improvement:** Express your commitment to continuous improvement. Let them know that you're always looking for ways to enhance the testing process and deliver even better results.

14) **Feedback Loop:** Encourage open feedback from them about your testing efforts. This shows that you're open to improving based on their insights.

Question 44. Could you walk us through the budget breakdown in your proposal and explain how the costs are justified in terms of the value your testing team will bring to our project?

Answer: Certainly, I'd be happy to provide a breakdown of the budget in the proposal and explain how the costs are justified based on the value your project will receive from our testing team:

Budget Breakdown:

1. **Personnel Costs:**
   a) Test Manager: Responsible for overall project management, strategy, and coordination.
   b) Test Lead: Assists the Test Manager in overseeing testing activities.
   c) Manual Testers: Create and execute manual test cases.
   d) Automation Testers: Develop and maintain automated test scripts.
   e) Performance Testers: Conduct performance and load testing.
   f) Security Testers: Conduct security testing.
   g) Usability Testers: Evaluate user experience.
   h) Domain Experts: Provide specialized insights if needed.

2. **Testing Tools and Infrastructure:**
   a) Investment in testing tools, licenses, and necessary infrastructure for both manual and automated testing.

3. **Training and Skill Development:**
   a) Ongoing training to keep the team updated with the latest testing methodologies and tools.

4. **Contingency Fund:**
   a) A buffer to address unforeseen challenges, changes in scope, or additional testing needs that may arise during the project.
      1.

Justification of Costs:

1) **Quality Assurance:** Thorough testing by a dedicated team ensures that the application functions as intended, minimizing the risk of critical defects that could lead to expensive post-release fixes or damage to your brand reputation.

2) **User Satisfaction:** A comprehensive testing effort guarantees a high-quality user experience, resulting in satisfied customers who are more likely to continue using your product and recommending it to others.

3) **Reduced Risks:** Effective testing identifies and mitigates potential security vulnerabilities, minimizing the risk of data breaches or security incidents that could lead to legal and financial consequences.

4) **Faster Time to Market:** By detecting and resolving defects early in the development process, our testing team accelerates the project's overall timeline, allowing you to launch a reliable product ahead of competitors.

5) **Cost Savings:** Addressing issues during testing is significantly less expensive than fixing them after deployment. Our efforts result in cost savings by avoiding emergency fixes and maintenance.

6) **Stakeholder Confidence:** A well-tested product put confidence in stakeholders, investors, and clients. This trust translates to stronger partnerships and potential investment opportunities.

7) **Compliance and Regulations:** Rigorous testing ensures that your application meets industry regulations and standards, safeguarding you from legal issues and penalties.

8) **Optimized Performance:** Performance and load testing ensure your application can handle user loads without performance degradation, leading to improved user satisfaction and retention.

9) **Early Issue Detection:** Our team's expertise allows us to identify subtle issues that might go unnoticed by less experienced testers, resulting in a more polished final product.

10) **Return on Investment (ROI):** The investment in testing directly contributes to a higher ROI by enhancing product quality, user satisfaction, and the likelihood of achieving your business objectives.

Question 45. As a Test Manager, how do you handle delays or changes in the schedule?

Answer: Handling Delays or Changes in Schedule:

1) **Proactive Monitoring:** I will closely monitor the project's progress throughout each phase. Regular status updates and meetings will allow us to detect any potential delays early.

2) **Risk Management:** As part of the risk assessment, I'll identify potential factors that could lead to delays and develop mitigation strategies. This could involve allocating additional resources, reprioritizing tasks, or adjusting the timeline. SEP

3) **Communication:** If delays are anticipated or detected, I'll communicate transparently with your team. We'll discuss the reasons for the delay, its impact on the overall timeline, and potential solutions.

4) **Revised Schedule:** If a change in the schedule becomes necessary due to unforeseen circumstances, I'll collaborate with your team to revise the timeline accordingly. The revised schedule will be based on the project's adjusted priorities and resource availability.

5) **Resource Allocation:** If a specific phase is delayed, I'll evaluate whether additional resources are required to catch up. This might involve reallocating testers or assigning more manpower to specific tasks.

6) **Change Management:** If changes in scope or requirements occur, I'll assess their impact on the testing timeline and adjust the schedule accordingly. I'll work closely with your team to manage changes while minimizing disruption.

7) **Contingency Planning**: I'll maintain a contingency plan that outlines the steps to be taken if significant delays occur. This might involve fast-tracking specific tasks or adjusting testing priorities.

Question 46. Can you call the base class method without creating an object?

Answer: Yes, we can but the condition is that:

a) Method must be static
b) Base class must be inherited by some other subclass.

Question 47. How do you iterate over the map?

Answer: We can iterate over the map using:
a) entrySet() method.
b) keySet() method.

Question 48. What's the difference between HashMap and Hashtable?

Answer:

Feature	HashMap	HashTable
Synchronization	Not synchronized (not thread-safe).	Synchronized (thread-safe).
Null values/keys	Allows null keys and values.	Doesn't allow null keys or values.
Inheritance	Inherits from AbstractMap class.	Inherits from Dictionary class.
Performance	Generally faster due to non-synchronization.	Slower due to synchronization.
Iterators	Fail-fast iterators (throw ConcurrentModificationException if the map is structurally modified).	Enumerator (legacy class, not fail-fast).

Question 49. Difference between String, StringBuffer and StringBuilder in table form with example?

Answer:

Aspect	String	StringBuffer	StringBuilder
Mutability	Immutable (Cannot be changed after creation).	Mutable (Can be changed after creation).	Mutable (Can be changed after creation).

Synchronization	Not synchronized (Not thread-safe).	Synchronized (Thread-safe).	Not synchronized (Not thread-safe).
Performance	Slower due to immutability.	Slower due to synchronization.	Faster (No synchronization overhead).
Memory Usage	Creates a new object when modified.	Modifies the same object, conserving memory.	Modifies the same object, conserving memory.
Example	java String str = "Hello";	java StringBuffer sb = new StringBuffer("Hello");	java StringBuilder sb = new StringBuilder("Hello");
Append/Modify Operations	Inefficient for concatenation due to the creation of new objects.	Efficient due to in-place modification.	Efficient due to in-place modification.

Examples:

String: Use String when immutability is desired, and you don't need frequent modifications.

```
String str = "Hello";
str = str.concat(" World");    // Creates a new String object
System.out.println(str);     // Output: Hello World
```

StringBuffer: Use StringBuffer when working in a multi-threaded environment and thread safety is necessary.

```
StringBuffer sb = new StringBuffer("Hello");
sb.append(" World");      // Modifies the same StringBuffer object
System.out.println(sb);    // Output: Hello World
```

StringBuilder: Use StringBuilder when working in a single-threaded environment and maximum performance is desired.

```
StringBuilder sb = new StringBuilder("Hello");
sb.append(" World");       // Modifies the same StringBuilder object
System.out.println(sb);    // Output: Hello World
```

Question: 50. Can you have overloaded constructors in the same class?

Answer: Yes, it is absolutely possible to have overloaded constructors in the same class. Overloaded constructors are multiple constructors in the same class with different parameter lists. The key is that they should have a different number or type of parameters.

Example: In the example given below, MyClass has four constructors, each with a different parameter list. The appropriate constructor is called based on the arguments provided when an object is instantiated. Overloaded constructors provide flexibility when creating objects of a class, allowing them to be initialized in different ways depending on the provided parameters.

```
public class MyClass {

    private int intValue;
    private String stringValue;
```

```java
    // Constructor with no parameters
    public MyClass() {
        System.out.println("Default constructor");
    }

    // Constructor with one parameter
    public MyClass(int value) {
        this.intValue = value;
        System.out.println("Constructor with an integer parameter: " + value);
    }

    // Constructor with a different type of parameter
    public MyClass(String value) {
        this.stringValue = value;
        System.out.println("Constructor with a String parameter: " + value);
    }

    // Constructor with multiple parameters
    public MyClass(int intValue, String stringValue) {
        this.intValue = intValue;
        this.stringValue = stringValue;
        System.out.println("Constructor with multiple parameters: " + intValue + ", " + stringValue);
    }

    public static void main(String[] args) {
        // Creating objects using different constructors
        MyClass obj1 = new MyClass();
        MyClass obj2 = new MyClass(42);
        MyClass obj3 = new MyClass("Hello");
        MyClass obj4 = new MyClass(10, "World");
    }
}
```

Question 51. Can we override the constructor? If not then Why?

Answer: No, we cannot.

In Java, the concept of constructor overriding doesn't exist in the same way as method overriding. Constructor behavior is not inherited, and therefore, constructors are not overridden in the traditional sense.

In Java, constructors cannot be overridden, and there are several reasons for this:

1) **Inheritance of Constructors:** Constructors are not inherited in the same way that methods are. When you create a subclass, it doesn't inherit constructors from the superclass. Each class must define its own constructors.

2) **Signature Matching:** Constructor overriding would require the same method signature in both the superclass and the subclass. However, constructors in the subclass must have a different name than those in the superclass, making it impossible to have the same signature.

3) **Object Initialization Order:** Constructors are responsible for initializing the state of an object. If constructors could be overridden, it could lead to ambiguity regarding which constructor should be called during object instantiation, especially in the presence of multiple levels of inheritance.

4) **Creation of Subclass Instances:** During the instantiation of a subclass object, the constructor of the superclass needs to be executed first to initialize the inherited members. If constructors could be overridden, it would complicate the initialization process, making it less predictable.

Question 52. What is the default constructor? Where we use default constructor?

Answer: A default constructor is a constructor with no parameters (i.e., an empty parameter list) in a class.

If a class does not explicitly define any constructor, Java automatically provides a default constructor for it. The default constructor initializes the object's instance variables with their default values (e.g., 0 for numeric types, null for reference types).

Once we define our own constructor, java will not provide default one.

Here's an example of a class with a default constructor:

```
public class MyClass {
    private int intValue;
    private String stringValue;

    // Default constructor provided by Java if not explicitly defined
    public MyClass() {
        // Initialization code can be added here if needed
    }

    // Other methods and constructors can follow
}
```

Use of Default Constructor:

1) **Object Instantiation:** When you create an object of a class using the new keyword, the default constructor is invoked if no other constructor is explicitly called.

   For example:

   ```
   MyClass myObject = new MyClass();  // Calls the default constructor
   ```

2) **Initialization:** The default constructor is useful when you want to provide a default state for objects of your class. It initializes instance variables to their default values, ensuring that objects start with a well-defined state.

3) **Inheritance:** If a subclass does not explicitly call a superclass constructor using super(...), the default constructor of the superclass is implicitly called. This is another scenario where the default constructor is utilized.

Question 53. How to get a number of elements in ArrayList?

Answer: It is very easy by using Streams in Java.

```
import java.util.ArrayList;

public class SizeOfArray {
    public static void main(String[] args)
```

```
        {
                ArrayList<String> al = new ArrayList<String>();
                al.add("Anand");
                 al.add("Amit");
                  al.add("AnandHooda");
                  al.add("Jivu");
                  al.add("Gunnu Hooda");

                long  size = al.stream().count();
                System.out.println(size);
        }
    }
```

Output: 5

Question 54. What is the difference between XPath and CSS? Which one is faster and why?

Answer:

Feature	XPath	CSS Selectors
Syntax	More complex and expressive.	Simpler and more concise.
Performance	XPath tends to be slower	Generally faster
Direction of Selection	Supports both upward and downward traversal of the DOM.	Primarily supports downward traversal of the DOM.
Text-based Selection	Offers powerful text-based selection using text() and contains().	Limited text-based selection options.
Element Selection	Can select elements based on their attributes, text, or hierarchy.	Primarily used for selecting elements based on their attributes.
Browser Developer Tools	XPath expressions can be evaluated in browser dev tools.	CSS selectors can be tested in browser dev tools.
Flexibility	Provides more flexibility in selecting elements based on complex conditions.	More limited in expressing complex conditions.

Which one Faster:

CSS selectors have been considered faster than XPath in terms of execution speed. The reasons for this include:

1) **Browser Optimization:** CSS selectors are native to browsers and are optimized by the browser's rendering engine. Browsers have dedicated engines for processing CSS selectors efficiently.

2) **Simplicity:** CSS selectors are often more concise and straightforward, making them easier for browsers to process quickly.

3) **Downward Traversal:** CSS selectors are primarily used for downward traversal of the Document Object Model (DOM), which aligns well with how web pages are structured.

XPath, on the other hand, supports both upward and downward traversal, which can introduce additional processing overhead.

Question 55. How to handle dynamic element in Automation?

Answer: Handling dynamic elements in Selenium can be challenging because these elements may change their properties or become visible/invisible based on various factors such as user interactions, page reloads, or AJAX requests.

Here are some strategies you can use to handle dynamic elements in Selenium:

1) **XPath and CSS Selectors with Contains:**
   Use partial values in XPath or CSS selectors using the contains function. For example:

   ```
   // XPath example
   driver.findElement(By.xpath("//input[contains(@id, 'partialId')]"));

   // CSS example
   driver.findElement(By.cssSelector("input[id*='partialId']"));
   ```

2) **XPath and CSS Selectors with Starts-With:**
   If the dynamic part of the attribute value is at the beginning, you can use the starts-with function:

   ```
   // XPath example
   driver.findElement(By.xpath("//input[starts-with(@id, 'start')]"));

   // CSS example
   driver.findElement(By.cssSelector("input[id^='start']"));
   ```

3) **XPath Axes (Parent, Child, Sibling):**
   Use XPath axes to navigate the DOM structure.

   For example:

   ```
   // Find the parent element and then navigate to the child
   driver.findElement(By.xpath("//div[@class='parent']/child::input"));

   // Find a sibling element
   driver.findElement(By.xpath("//input[@id='example']/following-sibling::input"));
   ```

4) **Relative XPath:**
   Construct XPath expressions based on the element's relationship with other nearby elements rather than relying on an absolute path. This makes the XPath expression more robust to changes.

5) **JavaScriptExecutor:**
   Use JavaScriptExecutor to interact with elements using JavaScript. This can be helpful when traditional locator strategies are not sufficient.

   ```
   WebElement element = (WebElement) ((JavascriptExecutor)driver)
   .executeScript("return document.getElementById('dynamicElementId');");
   ```

Question 56. How do you deal with stale element exceptions in Selenium?

Answer: A StaleElementReferenceException in Selenium occurs when an element that was previously located on the web page is no longer attached to the DOM (Document Object Model). This can happen when the DOM is modified or refreshed after an element has been found and stored.

To handle StaleElementReferenceException, you can use the following strategies:

1) **Retry Mechanism:** Implement a retry mechanism to attempt locating the element again. This can be done by enclosing the element location code within a loop and catching StaleElementReferenceException.

    For Example:
    ```
    int attempts = 0;
    while (attempts < 3) {
        try {
            WebElement element = driver.findElement(By.id("elementId"));
            // Perform actions with the element
            break;
        } catch (StaleElementReferenceException e) {
            // Handle the exception or log it
        }
        attempts++;
    }
    ```

2) **Refreshing the Page:** If the stale element occurs due to a page refresh or navigation, you can refresh the page before interacting with the element again.

    ```
    driver.navigate().refresh();
    ```

3) **Re-find the Element:** Instead of storing the element reference for later use, re-find the element when needed to ensure it is still attached to the DOM.

    ```
    WebElement element = driver.findElement(By.id("elementId"));
    // Perform some actions
    // Element becomes stale
    element = driver.findElement(By.id("elementId")); // Re-find the element
    ```

4) **Use ExpectedConditions:** Use the ExpectedConditions class along with WebDriverWait to wait for the element to be present, visible, or clickable before interacting with it. This helps in ensuring the element is in a stable state.

    ```
    WebDriverWait wait = new WebDriverWait(driver, 10);
    WebElement element = wait.until(ExpectedConditions.elementToBeClickable(By.id("elementId")));
    ```

5) **Wrap Actions in a Try-Catch Block:** Wrap the actions on the element within a try-catch block and catch StaleElementReferenceException. If the exception occurs, re-find the element and retry the action.

    ```
    try {
        WebElement element = driver.findElement(By.id("elementId"));
        // Perform some actions
    } catch (StaleElementReferenceException e) {
        WebElement element = driver.findElement(By.id("elementId")); // Re-find the element
        // Retry the actions
    }
    ```

6) **Custom Wait Strategies:** Implement custom wait strategies to handle specific scenarios where elements become stale. For example, you might create a wait strategy that handles AJAX requests or dynamic page updates.

Question 57: What is RFP and component of it? Have you been involved in it?

Answer: Yes, I had involved In RFP.

RFP stands for "Request for Proposal." It is a formal document issued by an organization to solicit bids or proposals from potential vendors or service providers. RFPs are commonly used in various industries, including government, business, and non-profit organizations, when they are seeking external expertise, products, or services.

Key components of an RFP typically include:

1) **Introduction:**
   a) Overview of the organization issuing the RFP.
   b) Background information on the project or services being sought.

2) **Project Overview:**
   a) Detailed description of the project, including its objectives, scope, and purpose.
   b) Any relevant background information or context.

3) **Scope of Work:**
   a) Detailed breakdown of the tasks, deliverables, and services expected from the vendor.
   b) Clear definition of the project's boundaries.

4) **Requirements:**
   a) Specific functional and technical requirements that the vendor must meet.
   b) Any mandatory criteria that proposals must address.

5) **Timeline:**
   a) Project timeline, including key milestones and deadlines.
   b) Timeframes for the submission of proposals and project completion.

6) **Budget and Pricing Information:**
   a) Any budget constraints or limitations.
   b) Request for detailed pricing information from vendors.

7) **Evaluation Criteria:**
   a) Criteria that will be used to evaluate and compare proposals.
   b) Weight assigned to each criterion.

8) **Proposal Submission Guidelines:**
   a) Instructions on how vendors should structure and submit their proposals.
   b) Required format, number of copies, and submission deadlines.

9) **Terms and Conditions:**
   a) Legal and contractual terms that vendors must adhere to if their proposal is accepted.
   b) Any specific terms and conditions related to the project.

10) **Selection Process:**

a) Details on how the evaluation and selection process will be conducted.

b) Information on presentations, demonstrations, or interviews, if applicable.

11) **Contact Information:**

a) Information on how vendors can contact the organization with questions or clarifications.

b) Contact details for the person or team responsible for managing the RFP process.

12) **Appendices:**

a) Additional documents or information that support the RFP but are not part of the main body.

b) Examples may include sample contracts, existing system documentation, or relevant policies.

Question 58: What are the various contents of Test Plan?

Answer:

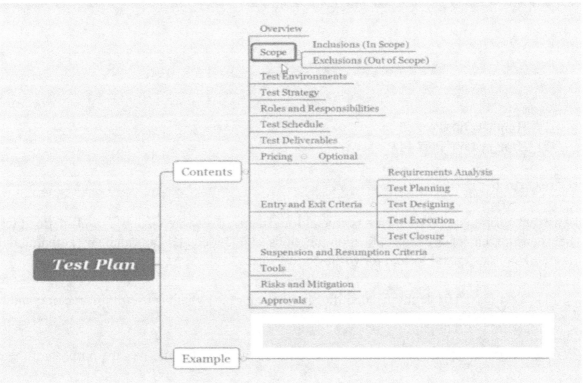

Question 59: According to you What is expected from Testing Team when a software needs to test?

Answer:

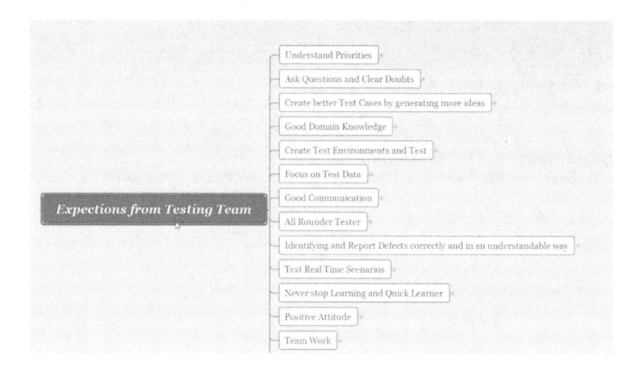

Expections from Testing Team

- Understand Priorities
- Ask Questions and Clear Doubts
- Create better Test Cases by generating more ideas
- Good Domain Knowledge
- Create Test Environments and Test
- Focus on Test Data
- Good Communication
- All Rounder Tester
- Identifying and Report Defects correctly and in an understandable way
- Test Real Time Scenarios
- Never stop Learning and Quick Learner
- Positive Attitude
- Team Work

Question 60. On Which port Htpp and Htpps are tested?

Answer:
1) Htpp test on: Port 80
2) Htpp test on: Port 443

Question 61. How do you define the format of writing a good test case?

Answer: Writing a good test case is crucial for effective software testing. A well-defined test case helps ensure that a software application functions as intended and can catch any potential defects or issues. Here's a general format for writing a test case:

1) **Test Case ID:** A unique identifier for the test case, which is useful for tracking and referencing.

2) **Test Case Title/Name:** A brief, descriptive title that summarizes the purpose of the test case.

3) **Objective/Purpose:** Clearly state the goal or objective of the test case. This helps testers understand the purpose of the test and what they are trying to achieve.

4) **Preconditions:** List any specific conditions or requirements that must be met before the test case can be executed. This could include data setup, system configurations, or specific states of the application.

5) **Test Data:** Specify any input data required for the test, including both valid and invalid data.

6) **Steps/Actions:**
    a) Provide a step-by-step sequence of actions to be performed during the test.
    b) Each step should be clear, concise, and unambiguous.
    c) Use active voice and avoid vague terms.

7) **Expected Results:** Clearly state the expected outcome or result after executing each step. This is used as a basis for determining whether the test case has passed or failed.

8) **Actual Results:** During the execution of the test, record the actual results. This is crucial for identifying any discrepancies between the expected and actual outcomes.

9) **Test Environment/Configuration:** Specify the environment and configuration in which the test is conducted, including hardware, software, browsers, and other relevant details.

10) **Test Pass/Fail Criteria:** Clearly define the criteria that determine whether the test case is a pass or fail. This is often based on a comparison between the expected and actual results.

11) **Notes/Comments:** Include any additional information, observations, or comments that may be helpful for understanding the test case or its results.

12) **Attachments/References:** Attach any relevant documents, screenshots, or references that support the test case.

Question 62. If you had to execute a big suite in a small window of time, how would you do it?

Answer: When you have a large test suite and limited time for execution, it's crucial to prioritize and optimize your testing process to ensure maximum coverage within the given timeframe. Here are some strategies you can employ:

1) **Prioritize Test Cases:**
   a) Identify critical and high-priority test cases that cover essential functionalities and critical paths through the application.
   b) Use risk analysis to prioritize test cases based on the potential impact of a failure.

2) **Categorize Test Cases:**
   a) Group test cases based on their nature (e.g., smoke tests, regression tests, performance tests).
   b) Prioritize test categories and focus on the most critical ones first.

3) **Parallel Execution:**
   a) If your testing environment allows, run multiple test cases concurrently to save time.
   b) Parallel execution can significantly reduce the overall test execution time.

4) **Automate Repetitive Test Cases:**
   a) Identify repetitive and time-consuming test cases that are suitable for automation.
   b) Automated tests can be executed much faster than manual tests and provide consistent results.

5) **Use Data-Driven Testing:**
   a) If applicable, use data-driven testing to execute a single test case with multiple sets of data.
   b) This can help increase test coverage without the need to create separate test cases for each data set.

6) **Dependency Analysis:**
   a) Analyze dependencies between test cases. Execute independent test cases in parallel to save time.
   b) Identify and execute critical test cases that act as prerequisites for other tests.

7) **Exploratory Testing:**

a) Conduct exploratory testing to quickly uncover defects in areas that might not be covered by formal test cases.

b) Leverage the tester's domain knowledge to find issues efficiently.

8) **Optimize Test Execution Order:**
   a) Organize test cases in a sequence that optimizes test execution time. For example, group test cases that require similar setups to minimize repeated configurations.

9) **Test Environment Preparation:**
   a) Ensure that the test environment is set up and ready before starting the test execution.
   b) Minimize downtime by addressing environment-related issues proactively.

10) **Capture and Report Defects Efficiently:**
    a) Set up a streamlined process for capturing and reporting defects.
    b) Provide detailed information in defect reports to facilitate quicker resolution.

11) **Continuous Monitoring:**
    a) Monitor test execution progress continuously to identify and address any bottlenecks promptly.
    b) Adjust the testing strategy based on real-time feedback.

12) **Feedback Loops:**
    a) Establish communication channels to quickly provide feedback to developers on critical issues.
    b) Collaborate closely with the development team to address issues efficiently.

Question 63. Java Program to reverse the element of an Array without the use of the reverse method?

Solution:

```
package interview;
public class ArrayReverse
{
        public static void main(String[] args)
        {
            Integer[] intArray = {10,20,30,40,50,60,70,80,90};

            System.out.println("Original Array printed in reverse order:");
              for(int i= intArray.length-1;i>=0;i--)
              {
                 System.out.println(intArray[i]);
              }
        }
}
```

OutPut: {90,80,70,60,50,40,30,20,10}

Question 64. Java Program to count the characters in the string(How many a, how many b, like this)?

Solution:

```
package interview;
import java.util.Arrays;
import java.util.Map;
import java.util.function.Function;
import java.util.stream.Collectors;

public class CountCharInString
{

        public static void main(String[] args)
        {

            String str = "Anand Hooda is a Test Manager";

            Map<String, Long>  Output =
Arrays.stream(str.split("")).collect(Collectors.groupingBy(Function.identity(),Collectors.counti
ng()));

            System.out.println(Output);

        }
}
```

OutPut: { =5, a=5, A=1, d=2, e=2, g=1, H=1, i=1, M=1, n=3, o=2, r=1, s=2, t=1, T=1}

Question 65. Java Program to count the Words in the String(like:How many Anand , how many Hooda like this)?

Solution:

```
package interview;
import java.util.Arrays;
import java.util.Map;
import java.util.function.Function;
import java.util.stream.Collectors;

public class DuplicateWordCountInString {

        public static void main(String[] args)
        {
            String str = "Anand Hooda is a good friend of Anand Rana and Pinky Hooda and
Hooda is Anand pet name";

            Map<String, Long>  Output =  Arrays.stream(str.split("
")).collect(Collectors.groupingBy(Function.identity(),Collectors.counting()));

            System.out.println(Output);

        }
```

}

OutPut: {a=1, Rana=1, and=2, of=1, name=1, friend=1, is=2, Pinky=1, good=1, Anand=3, pet=1, Hooda=3}

Question 66. Java Program to count the element in the a List?

Solution:

```java
package interview;
import java.util.ArrayList;

public class CountStringElement {
    public static void main(String[] args)
    {
        ArrayList<String> al = new ArrayList<String>();
        al.add("Anand");
        al.add("Amit");
        al.add("AnandHooda");
        al.add("Jivu");
        al.add("Gunnu Hooda");
        System.out.println(al);

        long count = al.stream().count();
        System.out.println("The size of List is =" +count);
    }
}
```

OutPut: [Anand, Amit, AnandHooda, Jivu, Gunnu Hooda]
The size of List is =5

Question 67. Java Program to find the duplicate elements from the ArrayList?

Solution:

```java
package interview;
import java.util.ArrayList;
import java.util.Arrays;
import java.util.Collections;
import java.util.List;
import java.util.Set;
import java.util.stream.Collectors;

public class DuplicateElements {
    public static void main(String[] args)
    {
        ArrayList<Integer> al = new ArrayList<Integer>();
        al.add(5);
        al.add(55);
        al.add(48);
        al.add(48);
        al.add(55);
```

```java
al.add(54);
al.add(54);
al.add(555);
al.add(486);
al.add(02);

// we can also write like

//List<Integer> aal = Arrays.asList(2,5,99,34,54,67,86,42,12,99,45,2,5,54);

System.out.println(al);

Set<Integer> duplicate = al.stream().filter(i-> Collections.frequency(al,
i)>1).collect(Collectors.toSet());
System.out.println("List of duplicate number is ="+duplicate);

}
}
```

OutPut: List of duplicate number is =[48, 54, 55]

Question 68. Java Program to remove the duplicate elements from the ArrayList?

Solution:

```java
package interview;
import java.util.Arrays;
import java.util.Collections;
import java.util.List;
import java.util.Set;
import java.util.stream.Collectors;

public class DuplicateElementRemove {

    public static void main(String[] args) {

        List<Integer> al = Arrays.asList(7,44,6,4,22,8,6,9,44,77,77,8,2,9,8,8);

        Set<Integer> duplicates = al.stream().filter(t-> Collections.frequency(al,
t)>1).collect(Collectors.toSet());
        System.out.println("Duplicate element= "+duplicates);

        List<Integer> NoDuplicates =        al.stream().distinct().collect(Collectors.toList());
        System.out.println("List With no Duplicates =" +NoDuplicates);

        List<Integer> sortedList =
NoDuplicates.stream().sorted().collect(Collectors.toList());

        System.out.println("Sorted List is =" +sortedList);

        }
    }
```

OutPut: Duplicate elemenet= [6, 8, 9, 44, 77]
          List With no Duplicates =[7, 44, 6, 4, 22, 8, 9,77, 2]
          Sorted List is =[2, 4, 6, 7, 8, 9, 22, 44, 77]

Question 69. Java Program to find the Factorial of a number?

Solution:

```java
package interview;

public class Factorial {

public static void main(String[] args) {

        int num = 5;
        long fact = 1;

        for(int j=1;j<=num;j++)
        {
                fact = fact*j;
        }
        System.out.println(fact);
        }
}
```


Question 70. Java Program to find the even and odd number in the List?

Solution:

```java
package interview;
import java.util.ArrayList;
import java.util.List;
import java.util.stream.Collectors;
public class fEvenNumber {

        public static void main(String[] args)
        {
            ArrayList<Integer> al = new ArrayList<Integer>();
            al.add(5);
            al.add(45);
            al.add(46);
            al.add(48);
            al.add(0);
            al.add(15);
            al.add(54);
            al.add(465);
            al.add(486);
            al.add(02);
```

```java
System.out.println(al);

List<Integer> even = al.stream().filter(i-> i%2==0).collect(Collectors.toList());
System.out.println("List of even number is ="+even);

List<Integer> odd = al.stream().filter(i-> i%2==1).collect(Collectors.toList());
System.out.println("List of even number is ="+odd);

        }
    }
```

OutPut: List of even number is =[46, 48, 0, 54, 486, 2]
List of even number is =[5, 45, 15, 465]

Question 71. Java Program to reverse the String?

Solution:

```java
package interview;

public class ReverseTheString {

    public static void main(String[] args)
    {
        String str = "AnandHooda";
        String rev= "";
        int len= str.length();

        for(int i =len-1; i>=0;i--)
        {
            rev = rev+str.charAt(i);
        }

        System.out.println("The reverse of String is = "+rev);

    }
}
```

OutPut: The reverse of String is = adooHdnanA

Question 72. Java Program to find the Second shortest element in the Array?

Solution:

```java
package interview;
import java.util.Arrays;
import java.util.List;

public class Second2Shortest
{

    public static void main(String[] args)
```

```java
{
        int[] x = {10,3,54,24,65,45,12,34};

    // Convert the Array in to List
            List<Integer> al = Arrays.asList(10,3,3,54,24,54,24,65,45,12,34);

        int secondShortestElement = al.stream().sorted().distinct().skip(1).findFirst().orElseThrow(()-
> new IllegalArgumentException("It does not have required element"));

System.out.println("2nd Smallest number is ="+secondShortestElement);

    }
}
```

OutPut: 2nd Smallest number is =10

Question 73. Java Program to find the size of an ArrayList?

Solution:

```java
package interview;
import java.util.ArrayList;

public class SizeOfArray {
        public static void main(String[] args)
        {
          ArrayList<String> al = new ArrayList<String>();
          al.add("Anand");
          al.add("Amit");
          al.add("AnandHooda");
          al.add("Jivu");
          al.add("Gunnu Hooda");

          long  size = al.stream().count();
          System.out.println("The Size of List is ="+size);
        }
    }
```

OutPut: The Size of List is =5

Question 74. Java Program to sort the element of an Array?

Solution:

```java
package interview;
import java.util.Arrays;
import java.util.List;

public class SortingOfElement {

        public static void main(String[] args) {
```

```java
List<Integer> al = Arrays.asList(2,5,99,34,54,67,86,42,12,99,45,2,5,54);
al.stream().sorted().forEach(t-> System.out.println(t));

    }
  }
```

Question 75. Java Program to find the elements that start and end with same Char in an ArrayList?

Solution:

```java
package interview;
import java.util.ArrayList;
import java.util.List;
import java.util.stream.Collectors;
public class StartwithSame
{
        public static void main(String[] args)
        {
            ArrayList<String> al = new ArrayList<String>();
            al.add("Anand");
            al.add("Amit");
            al.add("AnandHooda");
            al.add("Jivu");
            al.add("Gunnu Hooda");

      List<String> SameStart =  al.stream().filter(t->t.startsWith("A")).collect(Collectors.toList());
      System.out.println("Start with A ="+SameStart);

// we can use like this also. so one line will be less
al.stream().filter(t->t.endsWith("u")).collect(Collectors.toList()).forEach(t->System.out.println(t));
  }
}
```

OutPut: Start with A =[Anand, Amit, AnandHooda]
          End With u = Jivu

Question 76. Java Program to find the elements(Strings) that have length more than 8 in an ArrayList?

Solution:

```java
package interview;
import java.util.ArrayList;
import java.util.List;
import java.util.stream.Collectors;

public class StringCount
{
        public static void main(String[] args)
        {
            ArrayList<String> al = new ArrayList<String>();
            al.add("Anand");
            al.add("Amit");
            al.add("AnandHooda");
```

```java
            al.add("Jivu");
            al.add("Gunnu Hooda");

        List<String> test = al.stream().filter(s->s.length()>=8).collect(Collectors.toList());
        System.out.println(test);
        }
    }
```

OutPut: [AnandHooda, Gunnu Hooda]

Question 77. Java Program to find out the Sum of a number and also find count digit in the number?

Solution:

```java
public class ReverseTheNumber
{
    public static void main(String[] args) {

        int num = 879445;
        int revNum = 0;
        int count = 0;

            while(num!=0)
            {
                    revNum = revNum*10 + num%10;
                    num = num/10;
                    count++;
            }
            System.out.println("The reverse of the number is = " +revNum);
            System.out.println("The count of the digits in number is = "+count);

        }
    }
```

OutPut: The reverse of the number is = 544978s
         The count of the digits in number is = 6

Question 78. Java Program to find out the common elements from two Arrays?

Solution:

```java
package interview;
import java.util.Arrays;
import java.util.List;
import java.util.stream.Collectors;

public class CommonElement {
        public static void main(String[] args)
        {
        int[] arr1 = {10,3,54,24,65,45,12,34};
        int[] arr2 = {11,13,54,14,65,35,12,34};
```

```
            List<Integer> commonElements =    Arrays.stream(arr1).filter(a1-
    >Arrays.stream(arr2).anyMatch(a2-> a2==a1)).boxed().collect(Collectors.toList());
            System.out.println("The List of common elements = "+commonElements );


        }
    }
```

OutPut: The List of common elements = [54, 65, 12, 34]

Question 79. Java Program to find out the length of longest String in an Array?

Solution:

```
package interview;
import java.util.Arrays;

public class LongestString
{
        public static void main(String[] args)
        {
        String[] strings = {"Anand", "AmitHooda","JivuBaby","HarshitaHooda"};

    int maxLengthElement= Arrays.stream(strings).mapToInt(s-> s.length()).max().orElse(0);
    System.out.println("Maximum Length of string is ="+maxLengthElement);


        }
}
```

OutPut: Maximum Length of string is =13

Question 80. Java Program to find out the sum of all elements in Array?

Solution:

```
        package interview;
        import java.util.Arrays;
        import java.util.List;
        import java.util.Optional;

        public class ArrayElementsSum

        {
                public static void main(String[] args)
                {

                List<Integer> list = Arrays.asList(10,3,54,24,65,45,12,34);

                Optional<Integer> sum = list.stream().reduce((a,b)-> a+b);

                System.out.println("Sum of all elements is ="+sum.get());
```

```
        }
    }
```

OutPut: Sum of all elements is =247

Question 81. Java Program to find out the average all elements in Array?

Solution:

```
package interview;
import java.util.Arrays;
import java.util.List;

public class ArrayElementsAverage
{
        public static void main(String[] args)
        {

            List<Integer> list = Arrays.asList(10,3,54,24,65,45,12,34);
            double average = list.stream().mapToInt(e-> e).average().getAsDouble();
            System.out.println("Average of all elements is ="+average);
        }
}
```

OutPut: Average of all elements is =30.875

Question 82. Java Program to find out the square of each and every elements in Array?

Solution:

```
package interview;
import java.util.Arrays;
import java.util.List;
import java.util.stream.Collectors;

public class SquareOfAllElements
{
        public static void main(String[] args)
    {
        List<Integer> list = Arrays.asList(10,3,54,24,65,45,12,34);
        List<Integer> square = list.stream().map(e-> e*e).collect(Collectors.toList());
        System.out.println("Square of all elements is ="+square);
    }
}
```

OutPut: Square of all elements is =[100, 9, 2916, 576, 4225, 2025, 144, 1156]

Question 83. Java Program to find out the minimum and maximum number in Array?

Solution:

```java
package interview;
import java.util.Arrays;
import java.util.Comparator;
import java.util.List;

public class minAndMaxNumber
{
    public static void main(String[] args)
    {
        List<Integer> list = Arrays.asList(10,3,54,24,65,45,12,34);
        int maxValue =list.stream().max(Comparator.comparing(Integer::valueOf)).get();
        System.out.println("MaxValue is = "+maxValue);

        int minValue = list.stream().min(Comparator.comparing(Integer::valueOf)).get();
        System.out.println("MinValue is = "+minValue);
    }
}
```

OutPut: MaxValue is = 65
         MinValue is = 3

www.ingramcontent.com/pod-product-compliance
Lightning Source LLC
LaVergne TN
LVHW081804050326
832903LV00027B/2083